JUST AN OPINION

MURRAY DEAKER

JUST AN OPINION

HarperCollins*Publishers*

National Library of New Zealand Cataloguing-in-Publication Data

Deaker, Murray.
Just an opinion / Murray Deaker.
ISBN 1-86950-534-4
1. Deaker, Murray. 2. Sports—New Zealand. 3. Sports personnel—
New Zealand. 4. Sportscasters—New Zealand—Biography.
5. Radio broadcasters—New Zealand—Biography. 6. Alcoholics—
New Zealand—Biography. 7. Manic-depressive persons—New
Zealand—Biography. I. Title.
796.0993—dc 22

First published 2004
HarperCollins*Publishers (New Zealand) Limited*
P.O. Box 1, Auckland

Copyright © Murray Deaker 2004

Murray Deaker asserts the moral right to be identified as the author of
this work.

ISBN 1 86950 534 4

Cover design by Seven Visual Communications
Cover Photograph by Geoff Dale
Typesetting by Pages LP
Printed by Griffin Press, Australia, on 70 gsm Bulky Book Ivory

To Sharon, whose love, energy and enthusiasm are endless, and to Bill Francis, whose advice, patience and professionalism have determined my broadcasting career

Foreword

There was a time when, if Murray Deaker hadn't existed, no one would have invented him.

When I first met him 40 years ago he was engaged in a varied and, one might say, colourful career in Dunedin and all over the University of Otago. The son of a scholarly teacher and the sometime Dominion President of the Plunket Society, he seemed to his acquaintances, not all of them admiring, to be a combination of Brendan Behan minus the charm, Puck from *A Midsummer Night's Dream* and Moloch, the Canaanite deity who devoured babies.

Through an alcoholic mist he fell out of law school and into a good honours MA in history, and through the same alcoholic mist he fell into and then out of the hands of the provincial selectors in both cricket and rugby.

While he had a sober on-drive worthy of Ted Dexter his tight five play for his beloved Southern Rugby Club was epitomised by the *Otago Daily Times*, which said of one of his very few tries, 'Deaker trundled across the line.'

Departing the south for a teaching career in Auckland he was less a meteor than a jumping jack, from Auckland Grammar with John Graham (sacked) to Orewa College (let go in relief) to Takapuna Grammar, whose board felt they could not appoint him principal for fear of losing control over him (quite right, too).

But his hard-won sobriety and his big personality led him to a pioneering role in setting up the Foundation for Alcohol and Drug Education and then to the microphone and, alas, to the television studio.

He has been a very good mate to me and others, each of whom know that the words 'I need some help' bring an instant, warm and wholehearted Deaker to their side.

His coat of arms must surely be crossed bullshit detectors rampant on a cracker-barrel of sporting wisdom and if his heart is not so much on his sleeve as pumping in your face, where's the harm in that in these PC days . . .

Murray Jamieson
Coroner at Auckland

Acknowledgements

Bob Howitt at HarperCollins commissioned this book and then had to grapple with my handwritten scrawl. His countless decades as a sports journalist also helped to get a few of the facts straight. Most of our meetings took twice as long as they should have while we replayed the Rugby World Cup over and over again, but to no avail. The result was always the same.

Thanks also to Bill Francis for his help, advice and wisdom in reading the manuscript and suggesting subtle changes and to Murray Jamieson, even though he grossly exaggerated the truth in his foreword. Thanks, mate.

I am indebted to Sandy Myhre and Louise Callan for their generous editorial assistance.

The inspiration for the book's title came from the former Kiwi great and Warriors coach Mark Graham, who was furious with criticisms I made of him. In an interview with the *Sunday News* about my comments, he said, 'Opinions are like arseholes — everybody has one. The problem is this arsehole has his own radio show.' It amused me at the time and still does; hence, *Just an Opinion*.

A brief word

Much of what you're about to read is my opinion on various aspects of sports, sportspeople and sports administrators. I don't expect you to agree with all of it but I hope you agree with some of it. Most of all I hope it provokes you to discuss the real issues of sport fearlessly and honestly.

Sport should be passionately debated. A lot of what is included here has been debated on my radio and television shows. At any given time I believe that 60 per cent of listeners agree with me while 40 per cent disagree. Frankly I don't care — just as long as they listen.

One thing that continues to surprise me is that so many commentators and listeners view me as controversial and opinionated. I don't set out to be controversial. All I try to do is call it the way I see it.

None of the opinions in this book is expressed lightly. They are genuinely held — judgements I have reached from my own experience and the facts available to me, which are, for the most part, in the public domain. Hopefully they will create further debate because that can only be healthy for sport in any democracy.

Murray Deaker

Contents

World Cup cock-up

Sporting administration has known no worse bungle than the New Zealand Rugby Union's loss of the sub-hosting rights for the 2003 Rugby World Cup. This happened because of gross incompetence, unbelievable arrogance and extreme laziness. There are no words in the English language strong enough to express the disdain the culprits deserve.

At the top of the list put the names of the chairman at the time, Murray McCaw, and chief executive officer David Rutherford.

McCaw failed to inform the board that he had received a memo from Vernon Pugh, chairman of the IRB, on 18 November 2002, that made it plain that in demanding clean venues the corporate-box issue was alive. Under the heading 'Boxes', Pugh had written: 'Clean venues, including stadia and environs, is a fundamental term of the [agreement].' When NZRU councillor Tim Gresson, who had put the case for New Zealand's reinstatement as sub-host, heard about the Pugh memo, he realised all was lost. Unbelievably, McCaw had overlooked telling anyone of Pugh's memo for months.

Rutherford is equally culpable: he failed to allocate sufficient staff to assess what was needed to sub-host the event and to work on the event itself. At the crucial stage New Zealand had only two staff members involved: contract analyst Dean O'Shaughnessy and Lara Middleditch, an events-management specialist who had other responsibilities as well. John O'Neill's Australian World Cup 'team' numbered 16 full-timers plus a number of contractors brought in to handle specific tasks. Steve Tew, who had been a highly successful CEO of Canterbury and the Crusaders, was later appointed general manager of rugby and general manager of New Zealand's Rugby World Cup bid, a job sufficiently demanding for at least two, if not three, people. In his independent report, Sir Thomas Eichelbaum wrote: 'It seems plain that at least from mid-2001 a person of Mr Tew's capabilities ought to have had full-time responsibility for RWC [Rugby World Cup] and been supported by a greater number of staff.' If someone as conservative as Sir Thomas is prepared to state this so succinctly and plainly, it is imperative, when allocating blame, to find out who was responsible for this decision.

You don't have to look far. In March 2001 a report was put before the board recommending a separate unit be set up staffed by specialists. The board rejected it. Individually and collectively, the board was responsible. If Rutherford had been a stronger CEO he would have advised board members that without more staff the planning deadlines set by Rugby World Cup Ltd simply could not be met.

The NZRU board was ambivalent about the sub-hosting issue because so many of them were out of touch with grass roots rugby people. Too many of them were corporate types who had never felt the sprigs of a size-12 boot down their back when lying at the bottom of a ruck. Words like 'franchise' and 'product' and 'process' had replaced 'team' and 'game' and 'job'. The game's leaders were more interested in the bottom line of the accounts and couldn't give a toss about public opinion or rugby fans.

Some of those advising the board were even worse. One report the board commissioned stated, 'Unless the Rugby World Cup produces a substantial financial profit for New Zealand there is no reason to host it.' Try telling that to the rugby faithful from Kaitaia to Bluff. The thought of a board spokesman delivering that message to Colin Meads' Waitete club in the King Country, the late Vic Cavanagh's Southern club in Dunedin, Andy Leslie's Petone club in Wellington or Beegee Williams' beloved Ponsonby club in Auckland is laughable. No board has ever been so out of touch with its constituents.

There is a special magnetism associated with the World Cup, a vitality, a sense of occasion, even history, which make people want to be part of it. With the possible exception of Wales, no country is as fanatical about rugby as New Zealand. To deny Kiwis the chance to sub-host the major rugby event was little short of criminal. It is no wonder that overseas fans, players, officials and politicians shook their heads in disbelief at what happened.

In May 2003, I toured France and Ireland and took the opportunity to interview rugby correspondents like Ian Borthwick, a Kiwi who has been living in Paris for 30 years, and Tony Ward, the former mercurial Irish fly half who writes for the *Irish Independent*. Both were shell-shocked by the actions of the NZRU and commented how distraught many fans in the northern hemisphere were that the promise of seeing rugby in New Zealand had been denied them.

This sentiment was widely expressed, particularly by English fans at the Rugby World Cup. Many had planned to come to New Zealand, rather like pilgrims visiting the Promised Land. To these fans it was incomprehensible that rugby-mad New Zealand had turned down its chance to spotlight the 'second home of rugby' on the world stage.

When you accept that the World Cup attracted 1.87 million spectators, record TV ratings, a surplus of $A120 million and a profit for the Australian Rugby Union of $A50 million, you seriously question the business acumen of the NZRU board. You can add to that the innumerable other benefits. More than 120,000 Wallaby jerseys were purchased. No wonder adidas is rapidly losing faith in the Wellington Wallies. It has been estimated that English fans alone spent close to $100 million at the World Cup. You can only guess how many hotel beds, restaurant meals, hire cars, Air New Zealand domestic flights, trips across the Tasman, airport taxes, charter boats, golf green fees and wine and beer sales New Zealand companies and suppliers missed out on.

What we most missed out on, though, was showcasing our country to the world while promoting a sport we know a great deal about and play exceedingly well. New Zealand was denied the spirit, vitality, energy and enthusiasm that pervaded Australia, a non-rugby nation, throughout the World Cup. All the advantages associated with hosting the event — playing at home, the financial returns, experiencing the spirit the cup engenders, operating on the world stage and the influence on young players or those considering taking up the game — cannot be overestimated.

What compounded the problem was that the NZRU simply didn't do its homework. John Alexander, the CEO of Eden Park, revealed on my television programme that no member of the NZRU approached him until March 2002, after the original deadline, to determine the number of corporate boxes that could be made available. My inquiries suggested the same scenario applied at Carisbrook, Jade Stadium, McLean Park in Napier, Rugby Park in Invercargill, Yarrows Stadium in New Plymouth and Okara Park in Whangarei. Yet the NZRU said it had not signed the sub-hosting agreement because it could not secure enough corporate boxes. The truth was it hadn't tried.

When Chris Rea, a Rugby World Cup representative, visited Eden Park, he highlighted all the issues the NZRU should have been working through with Alexander, including signage, hospitality and media facilities. Alexander admits he was gobsmacked when told all his corporate boxes would be required. 'That was a huge shock to me,' he confessed. I interviewed Rea on radio at the time and he was insistent all the boxes had to be made available.

In his report Eichelbaum stated the NZRU knew from July the previous year that all the boxes were required. So why hadn't the NZRU moved positively towards achieving this? Was it frightened to approach the box holders? Were they worried about upsetting their corporate mates? Unquestionably, a large percentage of the box holders would have willingly given up their privileged status had they known it meant the difference between staging or losing the World Cup sub-hosting rights. It surely wouldn't have been too difficult for the NZRU to organise alternative seating in prime locations at the various venues.

What was already a shameful fiasco worsened when McCaw and Rutherford chose to level all the blame at Vernon Pugh and John O'Neill. At a disgraceful press conference, they began a series of stinging assaults that continued on *Holmes*. Here, Rutherford, for the only time during his tenure as CEO, chose to be forceful. He was so scathing of Pugh, questioning his leadership and guidance, that he cast aspersions on the chairman's character.

O'Neill's public reaction was simply to say Rutherford and McCaw had been unprofessional but deep down he was hurt and seething. He immediately instituted Plan B, which involved Australia proceeding as the sole host. It was a gutsy move, given that he had only $2 million in reserves and could have lost $100 million.

On 22 April, I interviewed John O'Neill on my Sky television programme, *Deaker on Sport*. He explained, 'I think the NZRU did not ever accept the fact that it was a sub-host union. It saw itself as fundamentally on the same level as Australia, and that is not implying any level of paternalism or big brother attitude on our part. What New Zealand was saying was that Australia has signed up to a certain set of standards but we want a different set of standards for our half of the tournament. That was never going to wash.'

Finally, O'Neill stuck the knife in by stating that New Zealand's rugby officials had become too big for their boots. Sadly, he was right. He could have added that they were tragically out of touch with public opinion in general and the sentiments of rugby fans in particular.

The NZRU, especially McCaw and Rutherford, obviously did not anticipate the depth of public feeling. In this, I believe I played a significant part.

For some months it had been apparent to me that the NZRU was putting little effort into successfully sub-hosting the tournament. After checking with a number of the CEOs I discovered that none had attended meetings with the NZRU. Nor had the major event organisers in the country been approached, something that should have been elementary.

All my dealings with David Rutherford suggested he was a man way out of his depth. Throughout one television interview he sweated profusely and had to be towelled down during the commercial breaks. Sadly, he was surrounded by buffoons more intent on preserving their own positions than assisting him.

The appointment of Steve Tew, a talented administrator and personal friend of Rutherford, came too late. Tew is not blameless. He badly underestimated the amount of work required and failed to appreciate the consequences. Perhaps his success in Canterbury had lulled him into a false sense of invincibility. McCaw gave the impression of being smooth and suave but unfortunately his rugby knowledge was veneer thin. His failure to inform the board about the Pugh email emphasising the necessity for clean boxes was unforgivable.

After McCaw and Rutherford denigrated Pugh and O'Neill, I decided to challenge the NZRU head on. Their attacks had effectively turned John O'Neill into Public Enemy No. 1 and when I brazenly declared that 'the NZRU has lost the sub-hosting through its own incompetence and arrogance' most callers greeted my words with scorn and derision. I stuck to my guns.

We arranged for O'Neill to come on the radio programme. As always, he was direct and strong. He did not hold back and suddenly the abusive phone calls stopped. By the Monday, Martin Devlin had come out strongly with similar views to mine and the tide was turning.

Two interviews on Radio Sport threw up red herrings. Andy Haden, the former All Black turned entrepreneur, argued that Pugh and O'Neill were in cahoots over the catering rights. O'Neill responded immediately, saying Haden should be careful of litigation and should either 'put up or shut up'. He shut up. Once again, O'Neill was showing that he could, as Sir Thomas Eichelbaum wrote in his report, 'play hardball with competence'.

Then Trevor Mallard, the Minister of Sport, made a total fool of himself when he suggested both Pugh and O'Neill should have bottles of cup sponsor Heineken inserted in 'particularly uncomfortable places'. Later, he met with Pugh in Sydney in what, not surprisingly, was a fruitless attempt to salvage the sub-hosting rights.

The television interview with O'Neill proved to be a major turning point and when one of his old sparring partners, David Moffett, the former CEO of the NZRU, came out shortly afterwards and said it was always understood the stadiums had to be clear of advertising and that corporate seats had to be provided, Kiwis looked sideways at McCaw and Rutherford.

Moffett told Reuters: 'I was involved in putting that bid together and there is no misunderstanding in my mind at all. We had an agreement with the ARU to share the Cup and I don't see what should have changed in the intervening period because everyone knows exactly what they had to do. It was well documented.' And that was it in a nutshell. Talkback turned 360 degrees with the general public now furious that they had lost out through the inaction and ineptness of both the NZRU board and staff.

Through it all Vernon Pugh remained silent, refusing to speak. I felt that the final doubters in New Zealand would be convinced only if they could hear and see him give his explanation. With this in mind, Greg Billings and I flew to Australia for the Rugby World Cup launch. When we arrived we were amazed to find that we appeared to be the only Kiwi journalists there. John O'Neill spotted me among the throng of reporters and came across, thanking me for trying to cover the entire World Cup saga objectively. I asked if he could arrange for me to interview Vernon Pugh. Between O'Neill and Chris Rea, the interview was set up.

It remains the only interview Pugh gave on the subject. He came across as sincere, caring and honest. He basically said New Zealand had not helped its case by its inability to accept the agreement Australia was prepared to sign. He wouldn't buy into my assertion that we were unlikely to ever host the World Cup again, being too poor to go it alone. 'Look, that's just not true,' he said. 'The NZRU is the third wealthiest rugby union next to England and France.'

Pugh acknowledged how disappointed Kiwis must have been and quite understood that he wasn't popular in New Zealand. At the same time, he pointed out that the IRB had bent over backwards to try and keep New Zealand in the loop. 'New Zealand has only itself to blame,' he said. 'Now it just has to get on with things.'

The interview was remarkably well received back home. The public accepted that Vernon Pugh had a job to do and the NZRU had all but made that job impossible. I was also able to report back to my listeners that all the Aussies I spoke to at the launch were enormously disappointed New Zealand wasn't going to be involved in the hosting. One former Wallaby coach, David Brockhoff, was heartbroken by developments. 'Listen, Murray, get this message through to your radio audience,' he said. 'We hate the situation we find ourselves in. All the blokes my age know there wouldn't be an ARU without the help we had from you Kiwis. We're deeply saddened.'

The findings of the Eichelbaum Report were telling. The key conclusions are worth listing:

1. The form of the bid for Rugby World Cup 2003 submitted by ARU and NZRU in 1997 was disadvantageous to the NZRU. The arrangements were open-ended and left NZRU in a vulnerable position. It is doubtful, however, whether the NZRU could have obtained any better deal;

2. Until the crisis, NZRU did not strongly press a case for Government funding, but it is unlikely any stronger request would have been successful;

3. A key factor in what went wrong was the breakdown of NZRU's relationships with the IRB/Rugby World Cup Ltd and ARU. A critical matter for NZRU to address is the rebuilding of those relationships;

4. From the end of October 2001 there was a known risk that RWCL might remove the hosting or sub-hosting rights;

5. The bid was made on the basis of 'clean' stadia, but at the outset

the definition did not include boxes. Formally, they were not included until October 2001 but NZRU knew from at least early July 2001 that RWCL would seek 100 per cent of the boxes. RWCL contributed to the problem by not defining its requirements sooner.

6. The crisis arose because when RWCL required delivery of all the boxes, NZRU was unable to deliver them, on account of previous contractual commitments made to boxholders with NZRU's knowledge;

7. NZRU had not taken any steps to obtain access to the boxes, relying on its chairman's belief that in November 2001 he had reached an arrangement with the chairman of RWCL, Mr Pugh, that a 'pragmatic solution' would be found;

8. Mr Pugh did not agree with Mr McCaw's understanding of their discussion. It had not been confirmed in writing and when asked for confirmation Mr Pugh had responded on 18 November that provision of clean venues was a fundamental condition;

9. The NZRU board was unaware of Mr Pugh's reply but otherwise was kept informed as critical events developed. Except for the public attacks on Mr Pugh, all significant executive actions regarding RWC were authorised by the board;

10. NZRU considered breach of the clean venues condition exposed it to a liability of up to $A10 million. A risk of that magnitude should not have been left dependent on an unconfirmed oral understanding;

11. In any event, the minimal proportion of boxes available would not have satisfied RWCL requirements. NZRU should have pursued obtaining boxes vigorously at an earlier stage;

12. Given a deadline of 8 March 2002 to sign the sub-host agreement in the form acceptable to RWCL, NZRU declined to sign and instead offered an amended document containing protective provisions. RWCL then entered into a negotiation with ARU, as it had said it would. RWCL recommended ARU's bid to host the World Cup alone. On 18 April, IRB rejected NZRU's submissions and accepted the ARU bid.

13. The NZRU board had adopted a cautious approach towards subhosting the World Cup. It was unwilling to do so at any cost. NZRU gave the appearance of not being fully committed to

sub-hosting the Cup. The perception was that it did not allocate sufficient administrative resources. NZRU's persistence in seeking approval to play NPC matches during the World Cup period was with the best interests of provincial rugby in mind but created the impression the NZRU did not properly value the opportunity to host the World Cup;

14. By 8 March, RWCL and ARU had lost confidence in NZRU. Although NZRU made every effort to recover its position it had minimal chances of success and these disappeared with the personal media attacks Messrs McCaw and Rutherford made on Mr Pugh;

15. NZRU did not have a viable strategy ready in case its 8 March counter-offer was rejected. If it was to continue to press a case for sub-hosting, the attacks were bad tactics. In any event, they were inexcusable, and damaged NZRU's credibility;

16. On 5 April, NZRU in fact signed the sub-hosting agreement in its unamended form, but it was too late to change the outcome;

17. No actions by Messrs Fisher or Gresson, in their capacity as New Zealand representatives on IRB (and, in Mr Fisher's case, a director of RWCL) contributed to the loss of the sub-hosting;

18. Although my report criticises actions and decisions by NZRU, other factors contributed to the outcome. Both the New Zealand and Australian unions played a part in the breakdown of relations between them. Administrative deficiencies of RWCL contributed to the final crisis.

After the report was made public, John O'Neill issued a statement that said, 'The principal conclusion is that the NZRU board was primarily accountable for the loss of the sub-hosting rights.' Meanwhile, the IRB slammed New Zealand officials for their 'consistent failures and wholly inappropriate behaviour'.

Whether you call it a mess, a shambles, a fiasco or a debacle, one stark fact remains: the NZRU was responsible and the board members rightly paid the price with the loss of their positions. David Rutherford resigned yet, staggeringly, agreed to explain his actions at a media conference. It was a black farce. Murray McCaw tried to hang in by resigning as chairman, hoping to survive as a member of the board. But common sense prevailed and he was asked to resign. The other board members, all of whom were sacrificed, were Rob Fisher, Steve Lunn, Tim Gresson and John Spicer, plus independent members Craig Norgate and Chris Liddell. The only individuals who survived were the Maori representative Paul Quinn (a former New Zealand Maori captain) and North Zone member Warwick Syers, who had only recently been elected to the board following the death of Brian Purdy.

Where did this leave New Zealand rugby?

Steve Tew survived. Whether he has learnt any lessons from this only time will tell. A significant number of the media believed he still placed Canterbury's interests first during his early years in Wellington and largely ignored the World Cup.

Jock Hobbs, who had first played for and then captained the All Blacks in the 1980s, heads the new board that includes such distinguished ex-players as former All Black captain Graham Mourie and former Southland and Otago representative John Lindsay.

When I remarked to one of the new board members that I was writing a book that would include a chapter on the loss of the sub-hosting rights he said, 'Deaks, if you think that was a shambles, you only know half of it. You've got no idea what we've had to clean up.'

The loss of the sub-hosting was felt most by those who love the game, the club members who couldn't afford to go to Australia for the great event. However, it is wider than that. World rugby missed out on seeing a rugby-mad nation embrace a tournament that it had every right to help stage. The game itself is poorer for that.

Deaker at the World Cup

When John Mitchell was appointed All Black coach in 2001, the rugby media breathed a collective sigh of relief. Here at last was a true rugby bloke from the grass roots of the game, a Mooloo man as earthy as the cow dung in a herringbone milker. How wrong we were. The only earthy thing about Mitch was that he treated all of us like cow dung.

It started with an early Paul Holmes interview that went radically wrong. Mitch didn't seem to know what he wanted to say and certainly didn't know how to say it. There were players milling around in the background, helping themselves to barbecue food, and the viewer was left with the impression the whole scene was a shambles involving a surly, inarticulate coach.

From then on, the entire media was treated with disdain as Mitchell withdrew into his laager. All journalists became the enemy and consequently the public rarely heard from the coach. When they did, they couldn't understand him anyway. He spoke in riddles, sounding more like a convert who had just attended a fundamentalist revival forum than a rugby coach.

Christian Cullen described him as 'a dick'. If Mitch were to return the compliment he would say Christian was a 'Richard' and no one else would know what he was talking about. Cullen's perception has a certain validity: when you did get the opportunity to interview John Mitchell, you were aware that he didn't trust himself. Every phrase, indeed, every word, he uttered was churned over in his mind two or three times before he opened his mouth. He had a new distrust for the media. The spontaneity that had marked Mitchell's time as Waikato captain had completely left him and he was acting as he obviously thought a coach should act.

His role models were the 1993 version of Laurie Mains and Clive Woodward, for whom he had been a most effective forward coach before returning to New Zealand. Mitchell had toured England and Scotland in 1993 as Mains' midweek captain, when Laurie was experiencing a dreadful time with the media. Woodward has pretty well always detested the press. After all, few of the Fourth Estate attended public schools. So Mitchell came into the job perceiving the media as the enemy. This would have been reinforced by staff at the NZRU, most of who are suspicious of the media, some to the point of paranoia.

Surprisingly, though, Tony Wynne, for many years an enthusiastic and energetic commentator at Rugby Park in Hamilton, was Mitchell's life coach. Wynne always impressed as a personable bloke with a good sense of humour who got on with a wide range of people.

Mitchell didn't seem to appreciate that the job he was taking on was vastly different from the one Laurie Mains had accepted and the one Woodward had moulded to his own requirements. Mains was *numero uno* but he didn't get to select his own support staff. Woodward is the boss, the CEO with total control, but he has the brains to succeed doing it his way.

In its debrief following the World Cup disaster of 1999 the NZRU attributed a major portion of the team's failure to the amount of power John Hart was given. He had selected all his support staff and, in fact, had the final say on all matters of importance. Everything required his seal of approval. That system is appropriate if the individual in charge gets every decision right. Of course, no one does. Not even the Pope is infallible.

The NZRU initially concluded that Hart was solely responsible for the failings of that particular World Cup campaign. And, to a degree, that was true. But equally to blame was the system he instituted because there were no checks and balances. Individuals appointed by Hart and answerable to him were hardly likely to criticise him or his decisions. The shortcomings of this approach were identified by former All Black captain John Graham, one of a group consulted by the NZRU.

Graham recommended the NZRU adopt the model that had been successfully developed with the New Zealand cricket team, the Black Caps. This structure gave the manager the power of a CEO with overall responsibility for the team, particularly regarding off-field activities. The coach, in turn, was responsible for training the team, for developing match strategies and for events on the field of play. Recently, this cricket model has been modified (don't forget, we're talking the Black Caps' model here) to give the captain complete power from the time the team crosses the boundary line. The NZRU agreed the cricket model was superior to the structure it was operating with the All Blacks and set out to make the necessary modifications.

Andrew Martin, a full colonel with the New Zealand Army where he was in charge of the SAS, was appointed manager. Strong-willed, well organised, determined, direct and honest, he encountered opposition from the start. Sadly, the media didn't give him a chance. He was tagged 'The Colonel' and his attitude was criticised before he even took up his post. He was always going to do things differently because he was given a fresh brief, but the NZRU never explained that to the New Zealand public or the media.

Martin had worked successfully with both Wayne Smith and Tony Gilbert and he invited me to meet with the three of them at his home in Remuera, Auckland, to discuss the ideal working relationship with the media. It was a very frank occasion. Smith asked me who I thought was the most influential person in the sporting media and I unhesitatingly said 'Me'. I may have been immodest but in light of the interview I conducted with Smith after the 2001 Bledisloe Cup defeat, an interview that led to his demise, it was a prophetic call. Andrew Martin didn't flinch when told he was detested by elements in the media and that this was largely because he was personally misunderstood. The media never grasped that he was now the boss, as authorised by the NZRU.

This meeting was a genuine attempt by a very sincere Andrew Martin to come to grips with the ever-widening gulf between All Black management and the media. It certainly led to a very open relationship between us.

John Mitchell, too, completely misunderstood the powerful position Martin had been placed in. Nor did he accept Martin's clear policies regarding alcohol and socialising, particularly where members of the opposite sex were concerned. Martin wanted to continue the clear, stringent guidelines he had successfully instituted with Smith and Gilbert but Mitchell embraced an entirely different philosophy. He believed in the seniority of the 'back-seat boys', that what happens on tour stays on tour and in latitude for the management team.

Martin and Mitchell were on a collision course from day one. They claimed, publicly, to admire each other. Privately, their views and philosophies were poles apart. Both are strong, determined men, firm in their beliefs, inflexible and downright pig-headed. A relationship that was simmering burst into flames after Martin criticised the personal behaviour of Mitchell and Deans on the tour of Europe late in 2002. When Mitchell became aware of Martin's report, he exploded with rage, giving the NZRU an ultimatum that 'either Martin goes or I do'. Martin left when the NZRU backed Mitchell, and that single decision is unquestionably the crux of all the later difficulties with Mitchell.

My first target, after the crushing semifinal loss to the Wallabies at the 2003 World Cup, was the NZRU. In *Deaker on Sport* on the Monday night I said that the NZRU was primarily responsible, that David Rutherford had been knocked out by John O'Neill, that John Mitchell was out-coached by Eddie Jones and that Reuben Thorne was out-thought by George Gregan. I added, 'NZRU officials should have a long look at themselves before they jump on the plane for their free trip across the ditch to the final.'

Shortly after John Mitchell's appointment back in 2001 a small group of journalists, including veterans Don Cameron, Bob Howitt and me, met the new coach at the Heritage Hotel in Auckland. It was a friendly, informal and thoroughly pleasant occasion that convinced wizened old cynics like Don and Bob that Mitchell would return the ethos to the All Black jersey. If Mitch could con the three of us, it's not surprising he ran rings around the interview panel. At the conclusion of the meeting, Mitch suggested to me that he would like to talk occasionally with a group of experienced rugby journos to review where we were all going. Needless to say, no such meeting ever took place — or, if it did, we three were never invited.

Mitchell is highly ambitious, completely ruthless and in my opinion, not a little devious. Upon his return from England, where he had built his profile in the Woodward camp and produced average results as coach of the English club team Sale, he took over the Waikato Development Squad. His stint there allowed him to meet NZRU regulations that required coaches returning from overseas to coach at provincial level before being eligible for Super 12 appointments.

The Chiefs job became available in 2001 and John Boe, who had represented the All Blacks and played more than 100 games for Waikato, had the front running. Really, it should have been no contest. Boe had compiled an outstanding record with Waikato, winning and retaining the Ranfurly Shield and guiding the side to an Air New Zealand NPC final. Unwisely, Boe met with Mitchell, concluding he had Mitchell's support for the job. Boe was excited at the prospect of two individuals steeped in the Waikato tradition taking charge of the Hamilton-based franchise.

Boe is now completely disillusioned. He has established not only that Mitchell obviously went for the job himself but that he actively campaigned against him. Boe, who coached Manu Samoa at the World Cup in 2003, is sceptical of Mitchell's coaching ability and he believes it was far too soon for someone so inexperienced to be pushed to the top.

Mitchell's other problem was that he surrounded himself with clones. His three major assistants, Robbie Deans, Mark Shaw and Kieran Crowley, were all products of rural New Zealand (not in itself a handi-cap) but they were all inflexible individuals and all distrustful of people from different backgrounds and with different personalities.

Robbie Deans is never wrong. Compromise and negotiation are syno-nyms for weakness in the Deans vocabulary. He is partisan and parochial, viewing the world through red and black glasses. Although he was not meant to influence selection, because of his status as Can-terbury coach, it is generally understood he was the individual with the greatest power.

How else can you explain the selection in the All Blacks of extremely average players like Mark Robinson, Sam Broomhall and Caleb Ralph? Worse still, he brought to the team the Canterbury pattern that had been successful for the red and blacks at provincial level but had lim-ited impact in a team chock full of flair players like Tana Umaga, Carlos Spencer, Doug Howlett and, in 2003, Joe Rokocoko, Mils Muliaina and Ma'a Nonu.

At first Mitchell embraced the Canterbury Mafia; indeed, he became their Godfather. It was ridiculous that Canterbury had up to 16 players in the All Black squad at one stage. It limited the options and strangled the All Blacks' development.

It also alienated the rest of the country and when Mitchell instituted policies to remove the team from public (and media) scrutiny at training sessions, this alienation became widespread.

But, unlike Mitchell, Deans at least had a track record. He had been outstandingly successful with both Canterbury and the Crusaders whereas Mitchell had achieved no more than average success with Sale, an English club team, and in his one year as coach of the Chiefs. His Chiefs team finished sixth in the Super 12, not bad by their standards but nothing startling in the context of a competition that until 2001 had been dominated by the New Zealand franchises.

A lot was made of Mitchell being forward coach to Woodward, but the English coach had a small army of helpers. If you asked the average fan who Woodward's assistant coach was during the 1999 World Cup, most wouldn't have had a clue. Mitchell got publicity in New Zealand about his status only because he was a Kiwi.

Mark 'Cowboy' Shaw was a tough, uncompromising All Black, a much respected individual who was often used as the team's enforcer. After a relatively successful provincial coaching career in the second division he became an All Black selector. Whatever his contribution in that role, it will always be overshadowed by the ridiculous comments he made to a *Listener* reporter in the build-up to the 2003 World Cup. Cowboy lived up to his nickname by suggesting the media were 'fleas', hardly the way to endear himself or the All Blacks to a group who can significantly shape public opinion.

Kieran Crowley, the former All Black fullback and Taranaki stalwart, coached Taranaki at NPC level in 2003 when the amber and blacks endured one of their most disastrous seasons. His team spent a season looking like the All Blacks in their semifinal against the Wallabies. Gutsy players rarely make good coaches and Crowley appears to fall into that category.

Deans, Shaw and Crowley were all peas from the same pod. They never gave the impression that they were prepared to compromise their views on how the team should be selected or prepared.

In one of the few interviews I had with Mitchell, I asked whether he would be calling on proven performers like Laurie Mains and Graham Henry. Once you waded through the mumbo jumbo of his reply, the answer appeared to be 'No'. Mains was initially consulted when he was coaching the Highlanders but as the laager tightened, he was squeezed out.

There was never any likelihood that Graham Henry would be asked to help. After all, Graham was never an All Black, nor indeed a provincial player. Rod Macqueen, the most successful modern coach, didn't represent Australia or his province but that fact often escapes the Mitchells of this world, and a number of former All Blacks.

It seems to me that any player who demonstrated individuality away from the field ran the risk of being eliminated. That was certainly the case with Andrew Mehrtens. The best first-five New Zealand has produced had committed the cardinal sin of questioning Deans at Canterbury and Crusaders practices and team talks. Deans wouldn't stand for it and began to drop him whenever he could. Carlos Spencer's outstanding form gave him the excuse he needed.

The public spin on this was that Mehrts was suspect on defence and couldn't run a flat backline. We were told that in the modern game the backline wouldn't function if the first-five hung back in the pocket, to give himself and his fellow backs time before the opposition loose forwards arrived. Yet for Jonny Wilkinson, named international player of the year and the standout player in England's World Cup triumph, this was the norm for a great deal of the World Cup tournament.

The first player any group of selectors should choose is the goalkicker. The second player introduced should be the back-up goalkicker. We currently have a fixation in New Zealand that our teams must score more tries than the opposition. It isn't the number of tries you score that wins matches; victory goes to the team that accumulates the most points.

Great eras are always associated with great goalkickers — Don Clarke of the '50s, Barry John in the '70s, Grant Fox in the late '80s and Mehrts for Canterbury, the Crusaders (and the All Blacks) in modern times. In fact, I defy anyone to nominate any significant era at provincial or test level when the pre-eminent team didn't possess a crackerjack goalkicker.

To leave Mehrtens out was just plain dumb and in my opinion Robbie Deans must take the lion's share of the blame for this. He had pushed for every other Cantab but it seems to me he couldn't handle the one who had given the red and blacks their edge for so long. In a word, the non-selection of Mehrtens was criminal. At half-time in the World Cup semifinal against Australia, when Carlos Spencer was so obviously struggling, wouldn't it have been appropriate to see Mehrts emerge from the bench? The Wallabies had stifled our Plan A. Mehrts was the ideal person to activate Plan B.

The other inexplicable selections were those of Ben Blair, Leon MacDonald and Ben Atiga ahead of Christian Cullen. John Mitchell told Cullen he needed to have his thumbs in a different position when he carried the ball up. Well, aren't they the same thumbs that dotted the ball down for 48 test tries, more than any other All Black has achieved? Blair was injured for most of the season and hardly played, although the selectors explained that he had a cracker against North Otago. Really! MacDonald had been concussed so many times he'd lost confidence. Perhaps that is why they decided to slot him in at centre, just to make it a little more challenging. And who was Atiga? A player of the future, obviously, but did the selectors genuinely believe he would make an impact at the 2003 World Cup? He was given seven or eight minutes on the field against Wales when he barely touched the ball.

The Cullen of 2003 was admittedly not the magical try-scoring ma-chine of a few seasons earlier. But the Paekakariki Express would still have left many of those others in his wake. Unless Atiga proves me wrong, I'd lay a sizeable wager that Christian Cullen will be remem-bered far longer than Messrs Blair and MacDonald (who's off to Japan, anyway) and the 'unknown fullback'.

Some will say I'm being wise after the event. Not so. I expressed my concerns early on. When Mitchell got the job, I said on my radio show: 'It seems amazing that an All Black coach can be appointed with such a weak coaching background.

'What has Mitchell done? He coached Sale to average results and left in strained circumstances. Waikato B for one year was hardly the background needed to coach the Chiefs and certainly sixth in the Su-per 12 in the sole year of coaching at that level is the weakest qualifications any All Black coach has ever had.'

The public reaction was predictable. One Waikato cow cocky rang to advise me to shut up and give the bloke a go. And for some time I did. Frankly, it appeared that Deans would do most of the coaching and his track record suggested this could possibly be a winning combination.

Those of us living beyond the Christchurch area had not heard the rumblings of discontent about Deans and his inability to get on with key players such as Mehrtens and Norm Maxwell. There was a suggestion he had fallen out with Nathan Mauger, who had passed his concerns on to the review panel. When challenged on this, Deans dismissed it: Robbie is never wrong. There was no possibility of this being investigated by a sycophantic Christchurch media, who in my mind remain the major public-relations team and cheerleaders for Canterbury and the Crusaders.

Despite the misgivings of the review panel, the NZRU turned a blind eye. In fact, it compounded the problem by allowing Deans to continue as coach of the Crusaders while co-coaching the All Blacks. They were an honoured couple: Mitchell was being granted absolute power; Deans was being granted unprecedented privileges.

Initially, the All Blacks were successful. They didn't require a lot of coaching because the players were merely swapping their Canterbury jerseys for black ones. It worked against the minnows, but would it be successful against the might of England or a fired-up bunch of Australians? Those of us in the media who wanted answers to these questions simply couldn't get them. Mitchell was aloof, distant and unapproachable. His media liaison officer Matt McIlraith, the former editor of *Rugby News*, was in an impossible position. His stock answer when you pushed him was, 'I can't do anything — you know what he's like.'

Three months before the World Cup final, I ran one of my best talkback sessions. I posed the question: What are the parallels between the All Blacks and Team New Zealand? I'm not in the habit of saving programme notes, but on this, and one other occasion, I did. Both demonstrate categorically that at least one member of the media was asking the hard questions, even if we couldn't get any of the answers.

Parallels between Team New Zealand (TNZ) and the All Blacks (ABs)
- High expectations
- No match practising (both teams wrapped in cotton wool)
- Other teams winning the PR battle (Alinghi owned large and influential segments of the media)
- TNZ defensive and colourless, although generally agreed not as bad as the AB management and selectors, who remain unapproachable and rude
- Both TNZ and the ABs had lost top personnel experienced in the business (Russell Coutts, Brad Butterworth, Dean Phipps, Murray Jones, Simon Daubney from TNZ, Christian Cullen,

> Andrew Mehrtens, Taine Randell, Jonah Lomu, Anton Oliver from the ABs)
> - Neither TNZ nor the ABs has settled combinations going into their events
> - Both TNZ and the ABs are untested
> - Both TNZ and the ABs face opponents more experienced and more successful, e.g. Coutts against Barker, Johnson against Thorne, Butterworth against Pepper, Wilkinson against Spencer
> - TNZ had half the financial resources of Alinghi. The ABs have less than half the resources and experience of England.

Given all these facts, realistically, what chance do the ABs have of winning the World Cup in Australia?

The All Blacks crashing out of the Rugby World Cup did not affect me to the same degree as losing the America's Cup had. Strange, really, because I'm a rugby man from the tips of my toes to my bald chrome dome. The approaching disasters with Team New Zealand probably passed me by because of my lack of knowledge of yachting. I'd made the silly mistake of believing what Team New Zealand's people were saying. However, deep down, to a rugby man, the All Blacks' World Cup preparation was a real worry. A month before the event started, I shared these concerns with my listeners on *Sportstalk*, opening my programme by listing the reasons I was worried:

1. The captain does nothing
2. The coach says nothing
3. The number one goalkicker kicks nothing
4. The new centre tackles nothing
5. The tight five destroy nothing.

Does this make it a Nothing team? I don't know, because I know nothing about the likely line-up, nothing about the team's current form and nothing about the team's likely tactics. When it comes to the All Blacks, I'm like a mushroom . . . I'm being kept in the dark and fed the proverbial.

The worst thing is I'm frightened I'll start to feel nothing about them. I desperately want them to win but I don't know anything about them. You could say I'm worried about nothing.

Considering that the headline in the *Dominion Post* after the semifinal loss was 'It's Only a Game', my final statement was prophetic.

Miles of newsprint and countless hours of radio and television have already been devoted to analysing why the All Blacks performed so badly at the World Cup. I believe you can summarise the reasons as follows:

1. John Mitchell was the wrong man to have as coach. His major faults were his inflexibility, his arrogance, his unwillingness to select players who displayed individualism, his preference for surrounding himself with assistants of average ability, his reluctance to use those with specialist knowledge, his complete inability to communicate with the public, the media and presumably the team and his obsession with total power.

2. Reuben Thorne was the wrong captain. A good provincial player, Thorne is barely adequate at Super 12 level and in the white-hot atmosphere of test rugby he was lost. Mick Cleary, the respected English rugby writer from the *Daily Telegraph*, nicknamed him 'Suitcase' because the team had to carry him. Thorne was incapable of changing tactics or inspiring his side. When the Wallaby prop Ben Darwin was seriously injured in the semifinal there was a delay of almost seven minutes before he was removed from the field. During that time the All Blacks stood around like dummies. Thorne didn't think to bring them together for a pep talk or even to share thoughts. It was a telling moment on Mitchell's 'journey'.

3. The team had no specialist goalkicker. The consequence of this was that Leon MacDonald played at centre, which caused additional problems. He couldn't tackle from that position.

4. The tight five simply weren't up to it. Even Chris Jack, the only genuine international forward among them, failed to recapture his best form during the tournament.

5. The All Blacks weren't match-hardened, which meant we hadn't learnt the lessons of 1999. Mitchell's men were wrapped in cotton wool and withdrawn from the Air New Zealand NPC and by the time they assembled at the World Cup some of them were gun-shy. Certainly, they weren't match-fit.

6. Tana Umaga was inexplicably left out of the semifinal when he was fit enough to play. Without him, the defence was disorganised and lacking in confidence.

7. Umaga's absence meant Carlos Spencer was unfamiliar with the attacking lines his centre was running, the result being an intercept try for Stirling Mortlock.
8. Australia played its best game for two years. It was, however, even better in the final against England.
9. The constant failure to recycle the ball quickly at the breakdown meant the team was never able to move the ball wide. Doug Howlett, who went to the World Cup billed the best winger in the world, was consequently nullified and his form dropped away sharply. The All Black forwards didn't know whether to commit to the ruck and maul or seagull out in the backline.
10. The All Blacks played what the overseas press termed 'pitter-pat' rugby.
11. They were soft, uncoordinated and ignorant of the basics. Rugby is a tough, hard, uncompromising, physical game. The ABs had none of those qualities.
12. It's rare to see the All Blacks operate without passion and intensity. Those essential attributes weren't evident at Sydney's Telstra Stadium.
13. The 2003 All Blacks lost touch with reality, with the media and with the fans. They eventually lost the plot.

If South Africa had been half the team it used to be the All Blacks would have been out of the tournament at the quarter-final stage. John Mitchell's 'journey' is over. He led us so far down the wrong path it's questionable whether we will ever again dominate the highways of old.

The America's Cup

Pete Montgomery and I share a common heritage. We are both southern men, both only sons, both influenced by strong mothers and both products of what we would fervently claim to be the greatest school in the country, King's High, Dunedin.

King's reflects what used to be the very essence of our education system. In the latest census on St Clair, the suburb from which a large percentage of the school's students is drawn, it was revealed that the average income was as low as $17,000 per annum with more than 4000 residents on income support. I strongly suspect that the statistics for neighbouring suburbs St Kilda, Forbury, Caversham and Corstorphine, which also feed into King's, would be poorer.

Yet the King's that Pete and I attended in the late 1950s and early 1960s produced a Rhodes scholar (Chris Laidlaw), outstanding surgeons like Garnett and Russell Tregonning, medical administrators of the ilk of Colin Mantell and leaders of commerce and economics.

It was a school where values, standing and status were learnt in the playground. The school rightly prided itself on a sporting tradition that produced All Blacks Ray Bell, Chris Laidlaw, Laurie Mains, Tony Brown, Carl Hayman and Tom Willis and a swag of Otago representative cricketers plus internationals Ken Rutherford, Keith Campbell and Brendan McCallum.

Most of all, it taught us a street sharpness and a sixth sense, so I should have been warned when PJ said to me late in 2002 that he'd seen the America's Cup destroy lives, ruin lifetime friendships and scar people for life. He was trying to warn me but the warning fell on deaf ears. The America's Cup would certainly scar me. And I owe PJ an apology for a most unprofessional piece of broadcasting when, on one of my programmes, I dared to question his integrity.

To say I became obsessed with Team New Zealand retaining the America's Cup is as much of an understatement as suggesting that Cantabrians have little regard for people living north of the Bombay Hills, that George Bush doesn't support the philosophies of Osama Bin Laden and that Australians play sport. From midway through 2002 until the America's Cup departed New Zealand's shores, I thought of little else, which was a strange attitude for a man who couldn't tell the sharp end of the boat from the blunt end and whose only yachting experiences were limited to half a dozen outings in the family 10-foot Seabird before some unscrupulous thief stole it from in front of our apartment.

I'd been warned but I chose to ignore the advice, to my personal cost. Unquestionably, my obsession led to my major depression in 2003 and caused a deep-seated rift with fellow broadcaster Larry Williams. The on-air spat may have given the public plenty to talk about, but it left our relationship in tatters.

For me, it all started that dreadful day at the Royal New Zealand Yacht Squadron when at a press conference organised to announce that Tom Schnackenberg and Dean Barker were taking over Team New Zealand, Brad Butterworth chose to read a statement explaining why he and Russell Coutts were leaving.

As statements go, Butterworth's bumbling, incoherent, appallingly delivered litany of half-truths rates right up there with George W. Bush's recent efforts about weapons of mass destruction in Iraq. He ended by saying he wasn't prepared to answer any questions because Russell Coutts was busy overseas. Now I knew that Coutts, Butterworth, Larry Williams and a few other cronies had been spending considerable time playing golf. They were busy trying to sink putts, not busy on America's Cup dealings. Amazingly, the collective yachting media was prepared to accept this lame request. I waited five minutes for someone to question him. No one did.

And so I went on to the attack. My first question was reasonable, I thought: 'Brad, this country has sacrificed a lot to give you and Russell a lifestyle most Kiwis can only dream about. Why have you turned your back on us?'

His answer was nonsense, something to do with giving the young blokes a go. Then he added, 'I thought I said I wouldn't answer any questions.' So what the hell was he doing there? Talk about red rag to a bull.

The 'interview' deteriorated: I interrogated Butterworth. Throughout it, staggeringly, he couldn't make eye contact. He rambled on, claiming all would be revealed when Russell came home. The cream of New Zealand's yachting writers appeared to be struck down with a severe case of laryngitis. Why didn't Butterworth come out and say, 'We've been made an offer we can't refuse — it will make us rich men'?

The New Zealand Rich List claims Coutts and Butterworth received $4 million each for defecting to the Alinghi camp and estimates suggest that the 'tight five' — the others were Simon Daubney, Murray Jones and Dean Phipps — among them cleared over $100 million. Who knows? Probably no one in New Zealand will ever know just how much they were paid, but whatever the amount was, it is only a fraction of what their departures cost New Zealand in lost revenue.

Three days after this farcical event, Russell Coutts arrived back in town. A press conference was set up at the Hyatt Hotel in Auckland and the same group of lily-livered yachting journalists attended, still suffering from their collective laryngitis. The conference was broadcast live on Radio Sport. Recently, I replayed it. Never have I been so rude, so emotional and so abusive while interviewing, but I have no regrets.

To me, Coutts and Butterworth weren't coming clean. Butterworth had gone down in my esteem after the previous session. Again, he seemed incapable of making eye contact and blamed everyone except Coutts. In his mind, he was the injured party. Well, if I never see him again, it will be a good thing. I completely lost respect for him.

Coutts was slightly different. During the previous campaign a mutual friend, Eric Faesen Kloet, had told me Coutts had a genuine gripe about Peter Blake and arranged a (secret) meeting between Coutts and me. We met at a coffee bar in Takapuna and Russell outlined the many difficulties he was experiencing at Team New Zealand. Basically, it came down to power and money.

According to Coutts, Blake and Alan Sefton had too much of both while he and Butterworth did the hard work for average wages. He outlined his difficulties with the board, claiming Sefton had Blake and the board locked up. He painted a picture of division, with the sailors being ripped off on the one hand by Sefton and on the other by the board. Russell said he also had a problem with some of the younger yachtsmen who were showing more interest in strutting their stuff around the Viaduct Harbour bars than doing the hard grind on board. In this, he was clearly correct. For some weeks, we had been fielding calls suggesting Team New Zealand members were expecting their shirts to bring all sorts of favours, from publicans to young women.

Eventually, it was agreed that I would attend a full Team New Zealand staff meeting and advise them on dealing with the media and their newfound fame. The speech had an interesting sidelight. By that time I was convinced the All Blacks would not win the 1999 World Cup. Coach John Hart had lost the plot and instead of focusing on rucks, mauls, tackles and passing, he was concerned more with image, promotion, media and politicking. I said as much. At the meeting were John Mayhew, the All Black doctor, and David Abercrombie, their physiotherapist. Later in the day my boss Bill Francis rang to say that Abercrombie had telephoned him, most upset that I had criticised the All Blacks and Hart. It highlighted the extraordinary power Hart commanded.

To everyone's surprise, Peter Blake turned up and sat in silence while I tried to motivate his troops. It was the start of a long and productive relationship with Blake. He didn't take umbrage at what I had to say, which included criticism of the way the administration was based on one side of Halsey Street and the sailors on the other. A representative of Social Welfare or the ACC must have been consulted to reach that decision!

From what Coutts had already told me, there was one horrendous rift in Team New Zealand. Coutts and Butterworth were plainly at odds with Richard Green, chairman of the board of Team New Zealand: they believed he didn't appreciate their worth or, if he did, he wasn't recognising it in tangible terms. According to some, Green could be arrogant and difficult to deal with, although on the one occasion I met with him I found him forthright, charming and honest.

Coutts and Butterworth were complaining to anyone who would listen. It was a concerted, concentrated attack that had been running for some months, although I had been oblivious to it. I first became aware of it when Green assured me that Coutts and Butterworth were telling anyone who would listen how Alan Sefton and Peter Blake were siphoning substantial sums out of the Team New Zealand coffers. According to them, the amounts being taken would prevent their boat being properly outfitted. They questioned where the television rights money was going, implying it was being routed into a private Swiss bank account. How ironic, given that it was Swiss multi-millionaire Ernesto Bertarelli who subsequently bought up the 'tight five'.

Initially, I believed Coutts. He can be a most persuasive individual who uses a conspiratorial style to assure his audience that he's relating the incontrovertible truth. And he'd approached me, not the other way round. He had me convinced that Blake was a smooth rogue and that Sefton was just as bad. But then two things happened to change my view.

Out of the blue, Sefton telephoned, requesting a meeting 'off the record'. This in itself was a major surprise, because five years earlier Sefton had accused me, among other things, of being a 'pain in the arse', implying I was the biggest single influence in degrading the America's Cup in the eyes of the average Kiwi.

Sefton took me to his Remuera home and opened the files. They were a revelation. Clearly, Sefton and Blake had earnestly tried to establish a succession plan for Coutts and Butterworth. It was crystal clear. All the major parties had signed a Mutual Understanding that empowered Coutts and Butterworth to set up an appropriate 'Charitable Trust'.

As an outsider looking in, it appeared a fair and equitable deal but still the rumours persisted. Blake, as always, was available for interviews. Nothing, though, could have prepared him for the ambush interview I conducted on Newstalk ZB. The line of questioning went as follows.

Deaker: I'm told there's bad blood, in fact a rift, between the sailors and the administrators in Team New Zealand. Is that true?

Blake: In every family there are squabbles and arguments. Team New Zealand is no different than any other family.

Deaker: Come on, Peter. It's much deeper than that. The sailors, I'm told, can't stand the administrators.

Blake: I'm sorry to hear that. We don't feel the same way about them.

I stopped the line of questions and we took a commercial break, during which Blake thanked me and said, 'I owe you.' Never one to miss an opportunity, I immediately said to him, 'Peter, when we win the cup, I'll ask you to come to Newstalk ZB and do an interview with me.' He agreed.

MUTUAL UNDERSTANDING

Joint Objectives

1. For Team New Zealand to successfully defend the Americas Cup and run a successful Event in February/March 2000 within the approved income and expenditure budget

2. To capture the hearts and minds of New Zealanders through a positive and united team spirit, fair competition and an ongoing proactive PR strategy

3. To provide for the maximum retention of key human and physical assets (including intellectual property and trademarks) beyond June 2000 (after all legal and financial commitments have been met), in order to support future successful Events and Defences

Personal Commitments

1. All parties will fully support and respect the present Team New Zealand Management and Board structure until June 2000

2. All parties will encourage open communication, mutual trust and cooperation throughout the team and will lead by example

3. Provided that the objectives and commitments are successfully accomplished, all parties support an appropriate charitable trust being established by Russell Coutts, Brad Butterworth and Tom Schnackenberg, to run the next Event and next Defence beyond June 2000

Extra Processes

1. The CEO to chair a regular Communications meeting to discuss PR strategy and team building (attended by all parties except sponsors)

2. Extra resources be put in place to ensure external relations with media and public are well coordinated and professional

3. A Transition Committee (attended by all parties and chaired by the sponsors) be established and meet regularly to cooperatively plan for a smooth transition to the new trust structure after June 2000 and, if necessary, make recommendations to the present Board

PLEDGE BY PARTIES TO THIS DOCUMENT

We, the undersigned, agree to work together in an open and cooperative manner to achieve the above objectives, to personally commit ourselves to respect each other's role in achieving these objectives and to support the extra processes to maintain mutual understanding

(Sir Peter Blake) (Bob Field) (David Balp) (Russell Coutts)

(Alan Sefton) (Douglas Myers) (Arianne Burgess) (Brad Butterworth)

(Richard Green) DATE September 1999 (Tom Schnackenberg)

40

After our successful defence of the America's Cup, Auckland became bedlam. Almost 80,000 tried to get near the viaduct and everyone wanted to talk to Peter Blake.

I arrived at the Newstalk ZB studio hoping that I might get a brief interview with Peter on his cellphone. When the reporters in the newsroom asked me who I had on tonight I replied, 'Blake.' The entire newsroom erupted in laughter.

'Forget that, Deaks. You're in the queue behind the BBC, CNN, TVNZ . . . your chances are zip!'

My producer tried to get Peter on his cellphone but to no avail. I left the newsroom and walked into the studio. Suddenly the producer's shrill voice came over the intercom: 'Deaks, look at the security camera and see who's just arrived at the front door!'

Sir Peter Blake was getting out of a taxi. We opened the security doors and a minute later the man everyone wanted to interview was sitting opposite me. He stayed the full hour, allowing Kiwis who had supported Team New Zealand to ring in their congratulations. Blake's word was his bond.

Another element emerged that illustrated how Blake was the team player while Coutts seemed to put personal interests first. Team New Zealand staged an open day that attracted tens of thousands of Kiwis eager to meet their heroes and secure autographs. I broadcast from Team New Zealand headquarters. Blake was there for the entire day and must have signed thousands of autographs but there was no sign of Coutts. The Kiwis who went to the open day were naturally disappointed that Coutts never showed up: it was an appallingly selfish display by a man still perceived as a national hero.

Douglas Myers, one of New Zealand's most successful businessmen, is among Blake's greatest admirers. He describes him as 'a sponsor's dream', a man prepared to go that extra yard to help the cause. It was Myers who revealed that Coutts and Butterworth broke Blake's heart. Blake had raised the bulk of the finance for the campaign, no mean achievement in a country hardly flush with corporate sponsors.

Yet Coutts and Butterworth refused to allow Blake to sail or even be on the boat. I'll repeat that: Peter was never allowed on the boat for which he had raised all the money. Even the strongest Coutts–Butterworth advocates, such as Paul Holmes and Larry Williams, must have difficulty explaining that away. Paul Holmes is usually savvy about public opinion. At the time he was struggling with his prostate cancer, Butterworth visited him and gave him a set of Team New Zealand gear. Tom Schnackenberg commented to me, some months later, that it was the best PR exercise Butterworth ever indulged in. Certainly, Paul's subsequent interviews with Coutts and Butterworth left the strong impression he strongly supported both of them.

Larry Williams is a good bloke, once one of my closest friends in broadcasting. I had tremendous admiration for the way this former traffic cop from Timaru had cracked it in the dog-eat-dog Auckland radio market. In my opinion, Larry became a PR agent for not only Coutts and Butterworth but also for Alinghi, who consistently fed him the inside oil.

My on-air arguments with Larry began in earnest the evening of the Blackheart lunch. I had been invited as 'first reserve' to speak at what became a highly controversial occasion. Dave Walden, an Auckland advertising executive, was the driving force behind the movement, a group of extremely enthusiastic and passionate Team New Zealand supporters. He approached Team New Zealand and asked if they thought Pete Montgomery would speak. Team New Zealand was un-sure where PJ stood. He was seen as a close friend of Butterworth and so Team New Zealand suggested that he should approach me. In hind-sight, it was a mistake for me to speak. I'm a broadcaster first and foremost, someone who should comment on events and happenings, not spark them.

Interestingly, the other speaker, comedian Mike King, avoided criti-cism for his part. Certainly, I didn't. The backlash came immediately, On my 5.40 p.m. promo slot with Larry Williams that evening, he asked if I'd attended the Blackheart luncheon.

'Yes,' I replied.

'You're pathetic,' was his response.

Then it was on for young and old. The 10 minutes that followed represent probably the most volatile radio between fellow hosts that Newstalk ZB has ever experienced. Some people said it was a set-up, designed to boost ratings. Rubbish! It was for real. Things have never been the same between Larry and me.

The America's Cup itself was a nonevent. Our team had spent too much time experimenting and too little time on the water. It was a two-horse race and we didn't even qualify for the runner-up medal. Coutts and his tight five made our afterguard look like kids learning to sail P-class yachts. It was hard to stomach.

One thing that remains vividly in my memory is the performance of the New Zealand media, particularly the so-called yachting experts. The Alinghi PR machine sucked them in. The *New Zealand Herald*, in particular, performed pathetically, and seemed to accept everything that Coutts and co. fed them. The paper used Julie Ash, an inexperienced journalist whose background was in netball, as their 'expert'. Unfortunately, Suzanne McFadden, who had done an outstanding job at the two previous America's Cups, had retired and her critical analysis, her ability to get to the core of the matter and her readiness to take a stand were sorely missed.

Alinghi's PR machine outmanoeuvred Team New Zealand's attempts at every turn. I had only one dealing with the Alinghi set-up. At the America's Cup ball, a feeble-looking fellow who told me he was a member of the Alinghi team approached me. I sarcastically enquired if he was the grinder. He said he was the head of PR for Alinghi and that if I was a Swiss journalist I would be told to be neutral. I said I could understand that because the Swiss let everyone else fight their wars for them and now they were doing the same in yachting, namely, letting others sail their boat.

He said there was just one thing he wanted to say to me. Before he did, I told him there was only one thing I wanted to say to him: 'Fuck off!' Well, he has. So has the America's Cup. And so have Coutts and Butterworth. Together, they cost this country billions of dollars and hours of heartache but most of all they cost us pride.

Never again will we trust any professional yachtsmen. Not that it will worry Coutts and Butterworth. If they had come out at the start and said, 'We've got an offer that's too good to resist, we're going for the money', we would have accepted that. Instead, they spent countless hours badmouthing the icon that was Peter Blake, blaming a board for underpaying them, grizzling that they were the injured party and selling their country's heritage for a truckload of Swiss francs. They may be brilliant sailors but their morals and standards are those of mercenaries. With a bit of luck, they will choose to remain in Switzerland and never return to New Zealand, a country whose finest yachting prize they forsook for the highest bidder. I hope never to encounter them again, a sentiment I'm sure they share.

Footnote: I received a most unusual Christmas present in 2003, a Swiss cuckoo clock. The attached card read, 'Murray, you're a difficult man to buy for, but somehow the clock reminded me of you — Brad Butterworth.' Good to know he hasn't lost his sense of humour.

Depression

People suffering from depression are gutless, spineless individuals more suited to the scrapheap than to being worthwhile contributors to our society. At least, that's how I used to view them. Strange, really, because since puberty I've been depressed four times, and those periods have largely shaped my life, leaving me shattered, disillusioned, insecure and frightened.

I'm writing this chapter more to assist my personal recovery than anything else. I'm deeply aware of the impact made by two of New Zealand's top broadcasters, Paul Holmes and Leighton Smith, when they spoke so openly and graphically of their battles with prostate cancer. In the wake of their revelations, I happened to be relaxing at the nineteenth in the convivial company of a cluster of North Shore cricketers at the picturesque Waitemata Golf Club in Auckland.

The discussion wasn't about who had carded what that afternoon, though I seem to remember that John Little, surely the most unlucky cricketer not to play for Auckland, had burnt up the course and burgled the Stableford prize, but almost exclusively about prostate cancer. Apart from the usual macho nonsense about the worry of having a finger inserted up the backside, the discussion in the clubhouse was remarkably forthright. Paul and Leighton's revelations resulted in all 12 guys who were assembled that day going for prostate checkups.

Not that this alone moved me to write about my trauma. I'm currently recovering from a devastating potentially killer depression. As I write this, I'm still in the early stages of recovery and not sure how permanent or successful this will be. Although one thing is for sure: I'll never be the same person again.

I'm now very aware of how many people suffer depression, most of them in silence, too ashamed to admit to what is generally perceived to be a weakness in their character. I may be many things, but weak is one characteristic that not even my most outspoken critic could pin on me.

As far as I'm aware, the only other high-profile sports person in New Zealand who has spoken about depression openly is former All Black John Kirwan. His book *Running on Instinct* contains a fascinating chapter entitled 'Black Dog', in which JK describes his battle with depression. At the time, I thought he was foolish to make such a revelation, that this was a private problem he should have kept to himself. All Black heroes should be powerful, strong, invincible. That's what we all believe, isn't it? Yet here was John Kirwan confessing he suffered from depression, even on the field while wearing the black jersey. I didn't understand then why he had to make it public, but I sure do now. John Kirwan is a fine man, honest, straight and transparent. By contrast, I'm complex, manipulative and insecure and, as I write this, frightened.

My sole purpose in penning this chapter is the hope that the honest sentiments expressed may help others, men or women, to face their personal devils. I hope my revelations may help some blokes at a nineteenth somewhere to open up about depression. We New Zealanders are great at discussing trivia — who should be in the All Blacks, whether Andrew Mehrtens or Carlos Spencer should be at first-five, whether Corne Krige spat at George Smith. But we struggle with topics like depression.

Depression nearly killed me. Without the help of close friends, I would probably be dead or totally mad. Certainly, without the unconditional love of my wife Sharon and the ongoing advice of two clever doctors, I would be on the scrapheap where society is so keen to deposit the 'weaklings' who suffer from depression.

Depression isn't new to me. I first suffered from it in the early 1960s. At that time, I disguised it by heavy, alcoholic drinking. Depression is similar to alcoholism in that it also affects the people closest to the sufferer, particularly loved ones who cannot help but be affected by the black cloud that surrounds the person they care for.

What is depression, or the Big D, as I prefer to label it? It's the pits. It's total despair. It visits without warning and it can be a killer. It's shameful, debilitating and frightening. It invades the mind, the body and the soul. Everything becomes a negative. Even the simplest tasks appear impossible. I was incapable of taking the top off a boiled egg. The sense of shame is all pervading, matched only by the sense of hopelessness and fear. We all need hope: without it there's little purpose in getting out of bed. But fear is the killer, fear of the unknown. Looking back, I don't really know what I was frightened of, but the fear was total, all encompassing and with me constantly.

The latest bout, my fourth, started, as so many depressions do, when I was on an extreme high. My medical condition causes me to suffer bipolar depressions, which means I experience extreme highs and deep lows. And during the summer of 2002–03, when the America's Cup was unfolding, I was riding high, then ploughing into the troughs of the waves like the boats themselves when confronting a piping nor'easter.

The America's Cup developed into a personal crusade; Coutts and Butterworth were my principal targets but I also viewed all the other defectors as traitors. I never recovered from the loss of the famous trophy. Although I'm an Otago boy at heart, I fiercely support the city in which I now live, Auckland. And it was heartbreaking to realise what the loss of the America's Cup was going to cost the City of Sails — millions, probably billions, of dollars. The yachting saga followed hot on the heels of New Zealand losing the sub-hosting rights for the Rugby World Cup, and those two shattering events pushed me to the edge; in fact, I was free-falling down the cliff, looking desperately for something to cling on to.

Bill Francis, the outstandingly efficient general manager of Newstalk ZB, who is a mentor and friend as well as my boss, tried to warn me. And my producer of 13 years, Greg Billings, looked on with great concern, unsure whether to back me or the company, or just hope the whole thing would go away. It didn't. I couldn't have soared higher if I'd been strapped to an out-of-control hot-air balloon.

Listeners and viewers of my two programmes were understandably bemused. Their presenter plainly wasn't behaving rationally, and my attitude polarised them. More than 500 letters of support and 20 of abuse were received. Talkback hosts are supposed to stimulate public reaction, but not quite to this extent. And the worst thing was, I didn't care. I was out of control, operating somewhere up in the stratosphere, or beyond. My wife Sharon assures me that the highs are worse than the lows. She would know, having endured me at each end of the spectrum.

The old adage reminds us that what goes up must come down. Well, I came down all right, with a thump. We were in Ireland celebrating our annual leave, but the holiday was anything but relaxing. I suffer dreadfully from jetlag, which triggered the bouts of depression in 1984 and 1990. Notwithstanding Air New Zealand's generosity in upgrading me to their luxurious quarters and treating me like a celebrity, my equilibrium was fearfully disrupted and while we were away I didn't sleep, except fitfully, for 19 nights.

I arrived back in New Zealand in early June a bloody wreck. Although I was relieved to be home, I was sicker than I'd ever been, so sick that I couldn't get out of bed. Everything was a huge effort. I couldn't make even the most basic of decisions. Choosing which shirt to wear represented a monumental decision. And my 60-minute radio shows, which normally take me less than an hour's preparation, were taking eight hours to prepare.

Normally, I'm a very positive person, capable of working harder and certainly more determinedly than most people. I make quick decisions, some of which inevitably prove to be wrong, but I drive them through to achieve a result. While I was in the depths of depression, reality became more and more distant. I indulged in navel gazing, concerned only with my most selfish needs and basic requirements. I was most interested in what there was to eat and when I could go back to bed. Suddenly things like the six o'clock news, *Coronation Street* and the daily papers, all of which I'm usually too busy to take any notice of, became important.

Although suffering desperately from sleep deprivation, which had me close to exhaustion, I dragged myself into the radio and television studios to perform. Surprisingly, the performances weren't that bad. They can't have been, because none of my superiors were aware of what thin ice I was skating on. Somehow, I manoeuvred my way through four weeks of programmes while grappling with depression. I guess it says something about my training and commitment that no one at the Radio Network or Sky Television picked up what was going on.

When you're in the depths of depression even the most mundane tasks become impossible nightmares. I completely lost confidence in myself and the last thing I wanted was to talk to anyone — which isn't exactly the ideal mental state for a talkback host!

Where this bout of depression differed from the earlier ones was that I didn't harbour any regrets or mope about lost opportunities. This time, I was completely sapped of energy and initiative and, as a consequence, had no time for anyone else. Others were obviously dependent on me, but I didn't care two hoots about myself so I certainly wasn't going to worry about them.

My world became smaller and smaller. First, it shrank to the size of our apartment, then to the confines of our bedroom where my work desk had been ill-advisedly placed. And finally it was no bigger than my bed. At my lowest point, I was reluctant to leave my bed. Had a close friend not insisted on visiting me, I might very well still be in it. And usually I have my feet on the deck overlooking Takapuna Beach each morning before my eyes are open.

Does depression bring on suicidal tendencies? The simple answer is yes: all thoughts became negative, black and morose, because I was so depressingly tired. I struggle to describe that tiredness. It was completely debilitating and horribly scary. It wasn't necessary to contemplate suicide because I was convinced that both my body and mind were on the point of surrendering.

There's only one thing worse than thinking you're going mad and that's looking into the eyes of the people you're talking to and becoming aware that they're absolutely convinced you're crazy. Hamlet's 'To be or not to be' played on my mind. I lost 13 kilograms in a month. I even stopped playing my beloved golf.

I hit rock bottom. How low is low? Low is when you can't taste your food. Low is when you no longer want food. Low is when you can't make love to the woman you love. Low is when you hate her for loving you. Low is when you despise the people you normally respect. Low is when you seriously contemplate the cliff face at Takapuna or the Harbour Bridge pylons. Low is when you hate yourself.

The lowest point of all is when your wife breaks down, because she can take no more, and sobs uncontrollably for an entire night before shifting to a spare room. And equal to that nadir is when you lie to a great friend like Forbes Worn, who helped you through your 1990 bout of depression, assuring him there is nothing wrong.

I don't know where Sharon found the strength to cope because my decline was so rapid. She always approaches life positively and tries to see the best in people. For weeks we endeavoured to weather the storm together, to keep it away from friends and the media. I continued to go downhill rapidly until that night when Sharon cracked. That did bring me to my senses momentarily, but I was far too sick to recover without medical help. What the long-term effects on Sharon and our relationship will be only time will tell. She believes she would have the strength to survive it all again. I don't believe I would.

My condition became very public after I surged to an extraordinary high. I'm certain it was drug induced. I'd been prescribed Aropax, an antidepressant, which had the same effect on me in 2003 as a bottle of bourbon in 1963. Now I was completely out of control, which led to two unbelievable performances on radio and one 'vintage' television show.

Kevin Shoebridge, a sailor who had returned to Team New Zealand after a stint with One World, copped the brunt of my overhyped attack. I asked him why any of us should ever again support Team New Zealand, given the history of sailors jumping ship. And in an editorial clip, I suggested, in strong terms, that Mick Watson would be better advised spending more time with the Warriors than posing for the society pages of the weekend papers. It didn't take long for Grant Dalton and Mick Watson to voice their protests to Newstalk ZB and I was off the air.

Frankly, I didn't care. I'd had enough. Thirteen years of being on the edge, pushing the boundaries, going where most sports broadcasters feared to go, had finally got to me. They could stick their job. Just who exactly 'they' were, I wasn't altogether sure. All I knew was that I'd had enough. I retreated to my bed and pulled the blankets over my head. I refused to watch television and I certainly didn't answer the telephone or read the newspapers.

It wasn't long before I became a news item. Speculation among the print media became ridiculous: Sharon fielded six calls from one reporter in a single day. The media's reaction wasn't surprising, I guess, given that I'd rarely been off air during the 14 years I've hosted *Scoreboard* on Newstalk ZB. In fact, on one occasion I presented 257 *Scoreboard* programmes in a row because there was no holiday pay clause in my contract. Some elements in the print media concluded I was back on the booze. That's when a photographer parked himself at the entrance to our apartment block for hours, obviously hoping to capture a shot of an inebriated Deaks.

Bill Francis was besieged with calls for two weeks. The whole situation revealed how rude and obtrusive some members of the media can become and what a depth of feeling there is between the print media and those of us in the electronic media.

The *New Zealand Herald* featured the story on its front page, outlining in detail what had happened on my television show: 'He delivered a diatribe to the camera as he called on the Prime Minister Helen Clark and Sports Minister Trevor Mallard to take a long look at themselves for not pouring money into rugby.' Such a statement may have represented a diatribe to a *Herald* reporter; by my standards, it represented a fairly tame statement.

Other articles appeared in newspapers throughout the country and the *Sunday News* sent Joseph Lose out to the Muriwai golf course to get 'the real story'. Joseph is a brother of Willie, a good mate who's beginning to make an impact in radio and television, and I've no doubt he knew what was wrong. But the article he penned was a beauty about the golf tournament and about epilepsy, the charity for which we were raising money.

Fortunately, Bill Francis was in Australia when I telephoned to tender my resignation. Equally fortunately, the first two people, beyond Sharon, to whom I announced my intended resignation, my sister Jan and my son James, would have none of it. Both declared their love and support and managed to convince me I still had something to offer as a broadcaster. More important, they persuaded me to seek professional help.

Doctors John Russell and Rob Shieff were the individuals who finally got me sorted out. John is more than my family GP. He's a friend, someone I've confided in for 23 years, a gentle, caring professional, a gentleman. Rob is younger and tougher, a no-nonsense product of that outstanding school, Auckland Grammar, and the Auckland School of Medicine.

There was nothing spectacular about their treatments. Depression, like alcoholism, needs time, and the sufferer must *want* to recover. I didn't want to wallow in my depression but, like someone lost in a maze, I couldn't find a way out of it.

No single event or product brought about my recovery. Aropax, the drug initially prescribed, was obviously not the answer for me and was replaced by lithium, a drug that acts as an equaliser, flattening out the extreme highs and deep lows. I was understandably reluctant to try it. Why would it work when Aropax had flipped me over the top?

Rob Shieff insisted that without lithium, or something equivalent, I would crack again. This warning ensured that I began scoffing the dreaded lithium pills as if they were chocolates. I resisted, though, when it came to sleeping pills. Neither John nor Rob could convince me of their value and it took an old mate to bring me to my senses.

When you're confronted with adversity, you need good people around you. Murray Jamieson has always been there. We went to Otago University together. We were more the Odd Couple than a perfect pairing. Murray succeeded with a string of degrees, was president of the campus and a Rhodes scholar. He was part of the establishment, a young man destined to succeed.

I was the chief shit-stirrer at the forum who was booted out of law school, fined a record amount by the vice chancellor for gate-crashing the physical education ball and managed to get myself banned even from the infamous Bowling Green Hotel which tolerated the most outrageous behaviour.

Yet Murray and I became great mates, a friendship that has survived almost 40 years. Murray is now the Auckland coroner, so I'm hoping not to confront him in any professional capacity for some time! Murray was overseas when I was in the trough of despair. I left a message on his answerphone and he rang the instant he cleared it. The following morning he walked into my home, although not without some drama.

On his journey home he had picked up a stomach disorder which manifested itself in a rather spectacular manner as he traipsed from his car to my front door. There he was, the coroner, sitting in our lounge wearing a suit top, white shirt, dress shoes and socks and a pair of my old rugby shorts, stressing how important it was for me to gulp down some sleeping pills.

He was right. I'd been reluctant to take sleeping pills because my body is so susceptible to chemicals. When I finally did yield and swallow a couple, I slept for 12 hours — which wasn't surprising, given the amount of sleep I'd missed out on.

Good people react in a natural way to the news that you've been suffering from depression. Inga Tuigamala, who helped decorate the All Black scene in the early 1990s, and David Tua, the only living New Zealander to challenge for boxing's heavyweight crown, accompanied me to Muriwai to play golf while I was on my huge high and before I was pulled off air.

On the journey home, with me at the wheel, Inga asked what was wrong. 'Man, you're so aggressive,' he said. 'It's like you're a different bloke. And if you keep driving at this speed, we'll all be killed.'

I gave an aggressive reply: 'Well, if you must know, I've been suffering from a major depression and I thought I was going to die.'

Silence filled the car. I looked in the rear-vision mirror: the man who went 12 rounds with Lennox Lewis looked as though he was about to break down. Meanwhile, tears were streaming down the face of Inga the Winger.

A few days later, Sharon and I escaped to Paihia. Inga rang Sharon on her cellphone to say he was on his way to Takapuna to see me. When Sharon revealed we were in the Bay of Islands, he told her he'd come up in a couple of days. He did. It was a Sunday morning and we played golf in the wettest possible conditions. Newstalk ZB had told the media that I was suffering from a virus. In Paihia, a group of Maori had been observing me as I played golf every day. On the day Inga partnered me, they were in the clubhouse following our round, and one said to me, 'Hey, Murray, how do you catch that virus?'

In my career as a sports broadcaster, I've been blessed to work with two ultimate professionals, Bill Francis and Greg Billings.

Bill is quite simply the best administrator the radio industry in this country has possessed. He loves radio, but he loves his staff more. I'm sure my colleagues Paul Holmes, Leighton Smith, Larry Williams and Martin Devlin would agree. Bill has helped them all in their rise to the top. Greg, without question the best sports producer this country has seen, is a mate, loyal to the end. And I've pushed him to the edge.

Those of us who suffer from depression need love, unconditional love, which can come only from our soul mate, someone we love and in whom we have total confidence. In my case that's been Sharon. No wife should have to go through what I put her through. I hope it won't happen again. But, given the mood swings of those of us who suffer from depression, who knows? What I do know, as one who has eyeballed the Big D and faced death, is that I couldn't have survived without the help and understanding of others. I never want to go there again. If I should, I just hope I have the same extraordinary people around me again.

Sharon's story

When Murray started writing this book, it was never part of the plan that I would contribute to it. It was his book, his story. But as he was applying the finishing touches, he and the publishers began discussing a contribution from me — what it had been like, what I'd seen and learned, as the man I love descended into months of hell.

At first I said no. I'm a private person. But Murray kept asking and slowly I began to change my mind. If he could find the courage to talk honestly about what had happened, so could I. Part of his motivation is the hope that these chapters will help others with bipolar disorder, and their families and friends. In the end, that became my reason for agreeing to describe my experience of this period; that, and because Murray asked me.

I've known Murray for almost 24 years and we've been married for seven magnificent years. I'd been aware for a long time that he'd had a couple of bouts of depression: one when he came back from overseas, the other when his first wife died. But I was unaware he'd also had one other, his first, as a teenager. With each of these depressions, time was a great healer; and with a balanced lifestyle he came right without having to use medication. Those experiences left us both totally unprepared for what happened this time.

The first indication that something was slightly amiss came during New Zealand's ill-fated 2002–03 America's Cup campaign. Murray involved himself personally, to an alarming extent. Surely, no one in New Zealand was more relieved than I was when the sailing ended. Never mind the sailors, by the final race I was exhausted and couldn't care who won and who lost. I just wanted this monkey off our backs. Murray

had developed tunnel-vision about the whole episode, virtually demanding that Messrs Coutts and Butterworth walk the plank.

A month after the America's Cup finished we were to travel to Paris
and then on to Ireland for Murray's television programme. Now Murray
is an extremely systematic and logical person. He doesn't enjoy long-
distance travel, so when we're heading overseas he organises his
No-Jetlag tablets, puts brown paper in his shoes, as many people do,
and compiles copious lists of things to pack and do. The night before
our departure, as Murray was placing items in his suitcase, he suddenly said to me, 'Do you think I'll need a pair of shorts?' As it was
about 26°C in Paris at the time, the answer was fairly obvious. I remember thinking, 'Uh-oh, we've got a bit of a problem here.'

We survived the arduous journey to the other side of the world but
once we were installed in our Paris hotel, Murray developed worrying
tendencies. First, he started to get disoriented. We'd strike out from
our hotel and before long it would become apparent that he'd lost his
sense of direction. Then we found he couldn't sleep. He'd crashed the
first night but from that moment on, sleep deserted him. He would go
the entire night without any rest whatsoever. We'd chat for a while,
then I'd drop off to sleep and no matter when I awoke, Murray would
be wide awake. We'd chat again, I'd doze once more and Murray would
lie there, anything but sleepy. It wasn't long before he began to lose
confidence and become withdrawn.

I was trying to understand, trying to come to grips with what was
actually happening and how we could manage whatever was bother-
ing Murray. After about three nights, I said, 'Murray, what's your major
worry? What's preventing you from sleeping?'

'Well,' he answered, 'my biggest concerns are the golf commitments
we've made in Ireland and the interviews we've set up.' (We were film-
ing a small documentary on golf and stockpiling rugby interviews to
use in the lead-up to the Rugby World Cup.)

His reaction blew me away. Murray loves golf: he's good at it and
handles interviews on any topic with consummate ease. That he was
declaring these issues a major concern meant we were in trouble.

From Paris, we headed to London, spending a couple of nights with
my son and daughter-in-law. While there, I said to Murray, 'Listen, I
think you're in trouble and you need professional help. You won't take
medication, so let's go home.'

Murray was reluctant to break the commitments we'd made, insisting on continuing with the project. I couldn't change his mind. So we flew to Dublin and drove through the countryside, barely surviving with Murray not sleeping a wink. We'd talk through the night, rise at 5.30 in the morning and go out for an hour's run. We didn't need to do that but it helped to fill in time.

Notwithstanding his sleepless nights, Murray never yawned during the day, which I found quite bizarre. Eating meant nothing to him and for someone who loves his food, that was another certain sign something was badly wrong. Yet through all these challenging days, I never once thought he would start drinking again, which demonstrates the strength of the guy.

Ireland was an endurance test, entirely lacking the spontaneity we'd experienced on other trips. It was very much business, with the solitary aim to get out of Ireland intact. We met some wonderful people, we played some fantastic golf courses and we stayed in some amazing home-stays in the most unusual and beautiful settings, yet we didn't enjoy any of it. For us, it was as bland, colourless and as unexciting as a plate of porridge.

Back home in Takapuna, Murray went to his GP, who prescribed a medication that finally helped him sleep. But unbeknown to both of us, the depression was accelerating.

There were days when he would say, 'Do you think I need to wear a singlet?' or 'I don't think I can get out of bed.' He was back into his radio programme with Newstalk ZB, but it would take him the whole day to prepare for the one-hour show. Normally, he's superbly efficient and completes the preparation with ease. Now after five hours he'd have two paragraphs written down and both of them crossed out! Normally Murray is a gifted writer, the words flowing from his pen. That he was agonising in this way meant he was really was in trouble. And things were no better at the radio station, where he had no confidence in his decisions or statements. Life was becoming terribly painful for him.

As his health deteriorated, his greatest fear was that he would lose the hosting of his radio or television shows. That was the reason we endeavoured to contain the problem. It wasn't the stigma. It was about recovering from this dreadful malaise that had gripped him. Initially, I believed he would soon rebound from his depression, as he had on the two previous occasions I knew about. Time would heal; tomorrow would be a better day than today. In fact, each day was worse than the one before. We were living a nightmare.

One positive came out of it. When Murray was so deeply depressed, it brought us together because it felt as though it was us against the world. We talked through all our problems. Because Murray was so down, I used all the strength I could muster to give him as much love and support as possible.

His GP suggested he go to a stress counsellor, but I was pretty negative about that. It seemed a bit New Age for me. Personally, I felt he should see a psychiatrist who could advise on and manage his medication. His reaction to that suggestion was typical: 'Murray Deaker doesn't do psychiatrists.' So we continued seeing the GP until eventually he referred Murray to a psychiatrist. By now, Murray, in despair and after speaking with his son, accepted the suggestion. He knew he needed professional help. The psychiatrist prescribed medication to which Murray reacted strongly, spectacularly so. It catapulted him from the depths of depression and sent him flying high.

This was an extremely difficult time for me, although probably not so hard for Murray. He thrives on highs — he possesses a personality that's over the top anyway — and now he was frenetic, go-go-go all the time. He was constantly on the phone, organising events. Once, he had three meetings going simultaneously: he was planning for the Rugby World Cup, he was in on the Fight for Life and he was scheduling a charity golf match. Just one of those events would be enough for most people. And as if that wasn't enough, he began furiously writing chapters for a new book, the one you're reading now. He assured the publishers that the handwritten manuscript, all 70,000-odd words, could be completed inside a month!

During this frenetic phase he was surviving on a couple of hours sleep a night. Unfortunately, I wasn't. I was now desperately tired from trying to keep track of what he was up to. The safety angle became a stress factor for me because during his depression he had alluded to suicide.

I'd never experienced Murray on this roller-coaster high where he was operating as though he controlled the world, wanting action all the time, parties, people around him. It was exhausting, scary. When I compared the man I'd known before with the one who was now on this super adrenaline high, I discovered components of his personality and behaviour that were totally foreign to me.

This wasn't the Murray I knew. This one swore, told lies, gambled and displayed almost total intolerance of other people's opinions because his views were always correct. God and right were on his side. Because I felt a compulsive need to know what was going on, I tried to be with him as much as possible, first, to help ensure his safety and, second, to oversee the deals he was setting up. I wanted to make sure they had credibility and could be delivered on. Remarkably, all things considered, he managed very well. I just didn't want him firing off faxes to the NZRU delivering hard, home truths that would have been better left unsaid.

I also felt that if I'd stopped caring about his behaviour it would have had a negative impact on our relationship. I never stopped caring, even when my eyes were heavy and ringed from worry and sleep deprivation.

The most frightening time, I believe, was when I looked into Murray's eyes and didn't see the love that had always been there. That hurt. When he hit the nadir of his depression, we worked together. But when he soared off on this unbelievable high, I became the jailer, the person dragging him back. He was not only into deals, he was spending a lot of money. He was buying people gifts all the time and was heading for the casino when he told me he was attending a meeting. While he'd punted many years previously, he'd never bothered about casinos.

So he was largely ignoring me because he knew I would disapprove of his behaviour.

For example, he bought a table for the Fight of Life and invited a whole cluster of guests along. I was unaware of this arrangement until a couple who couldn't make it telephoned to advise they wouldn't be attending. Life was full of surprises at the time and this one, I felt, wasn't in Murray's best interests at all. The Fight for Life setting, abounding in testosterone and alcohol, would have provided the worst possible environment for an excitable Murray, and he would have been surrounded by league people and others he had criticised on his radio and TV programmes. They would have been right in his face. Fortunately, he permitted me to extricate him from that engagement.

We were still seeing the psychiatrist and it was obvious the drugs Murray was on needed to be altered. Medical advice was also that

58

Murray would make better progress if we were away from Auckland where the media were hassling us. He was constantly on the phone and his home environment was only serving to accentuate his bizarre behaviour. So after the medication was changed we went to stay with my parents in Paihia for eight days. The idea was to relax, play golf and contemplate the future. Both the doctors and I wanted Murray to leave his mobile phone at home, and he agreed. But the first morning in Paihia he went out and bought a new one, insisting he couldn't exist without it.

When we returned to Auckland, he was still out of control, so I decided a trip to Queenstown would be appropriate. The day before our flight south, we were sitting in the living room and Murray fell quiet. It was as if a hot-air balloon, having descended to earth, was suddenly contracting. His eyes were getting heavier and heavier and over a period of two hours he came right down. He took himself off to bed early that evening and I had to wake him at 6.30 the next morning so we could catch our flight. I spent the rest of that day trying to keep him awake. It was as if, after free-falling from a great height, his body was saying enough's enough.

When we arrived in Queenstown he slept all the way to the hotel. He had committed himself to do a crossover with Larry Williams on Newstalk ZB, which he honoured. But his speech was slurred and his comments almost unintelligible and I doubted they would have been able to use any of it. Murray slept solidly through till seven o'clock the next morning, unaware when he woke whether it was night or day. He'd come off the high and started down the road to recovery.

Murray hates medication with a passion. When he was on the high he ate little and benefited physically. But once he started taking lithium his weight increased, something he loathes. He'd been writing copious notes on anything and everything, but the lithium slowed him down. He felt it affected his creativity and energy levels. Despite this, he started to make progress and resumed his radio work. Every day, though, he would complain bitterly at having to be on medication.

Then one day he declared he'd taken himself off the lithium. Unbeknown to me, he hadn't been using it for three weeks, claiming he was feeling so much better without it. Murray was content, but I was scared. Everything I'd read emphasised the importance of continuing with the medication. Nothing I said could convince Murray that he was treading a tightrope. He could remember events from his depressive period, and how scared he was, but he recalled almost nothing from when he was flying high. He told me if I saw him heading that way again I should alert him and he would resume his medication. The theory was fine but I knew that the reality could be dramatically different. From vivid recent experience, I knew I was the last person he would listen to once he'd become 'airborne' again. I told him it wouldn't work.

Within a month I could see signs that he was winding up again and I didn't think we could possibly survive another onslaught. He was getting frenetic again, committing himself to events without consulting me. Previously, we had always been fantastic communicators. He'd stopped visiting the psychiatrist and I was deeply concerned. Close friends were worried as well, so when he returned from the Rugby World Cup, Bill Francis and I had a meeting with Murray and the GP and Murray agreed to go back on the lithium. Once again, he hated it.

'You hate it so much and yet you know you've got an illness,' I said to him. 'If you were a diabetic, you'd take insulin. If you had cancer you'd surely use the drugs prescribed for you. You have a bipolar depressive disorder and lithium is part of the recovery. If you hate it so much, why are you taking it?'

He replied, 'Sharon, the only reason I'm taking it is because you're on my case so much. I couldn't take that any more.'

Obviously, the taking of lithium had become a negative in our relationship: Murray resented having to take it and I was the one insisting he did so. When Murray's depressive condition first manifested itself, I knew nothing about bipolar disorder, so I looked for books that would enlighten me, and I talked to doctors.

One book I came across could only be described as amazing. It's *An Unquiet Mind* by Kay Redfield Jamison. I instantly identified with it — the signs and symptoms, the impact that this illness has on relationships and the importance of medication. She recorded that a large percentage of individuals suffering from depression came unstuck when they stopped taking their medication.

Murray was still reluctant to resume his medication so I rang his psychiatrist. I thought he would have a few tricks up his sleeve, or some suggestions about how we would get Murray back to see him.

His response was, 'Sharon, he knows that he's bipolar. He knows that the medication is essential. And it may well be that he has to come unstuck three or four times before he actually accepts the inevitability of the situation.'

Being depressive is very like being an alcoholic. You can't give up alcohol for somebody else. You can only give it up for yourself. Murray couldn't stay on medication for my sake. He was going to have to do it for himself.

This is an illness that takes a husband-and-wife relationship and batters it around mercilessly. When Murray first became ill while we were overseas, and following our return home, our relationship was reinforced because we both needed each other. We communicated really well. But when Murray blasted off into outer space life became incredibly difficult. That closeness disintegrated. Now I was perceived as the monster who was restricting his fun.

Aspects of Murray's behaviour at the time were so hurtful I had to keep reminding myself that this was a sick person, not the man I loved. That way I could handle it. Murray is big and loud, but he's a softy underneath, and gentle. But when he was going through that phase, that softness was missing. Then the added drama of the day when he couldn't get out of bed — well, that threw me.

A couple of people suggested that to survive I might need help. But I always knew I had enough strength for both of us. I always knew we'd come out of it. Murray didn't, but I did. When our life was at its most chaotic, and I was wondering what new surprises each day had in store, I never believed I would be confronted with more than I could handle. That was what got me through.

And we did receive help and support, both of us. The kids were fantastic.

Initially, Murray and I sought to contain the whole thing, so we didn't see much of the family when we returned from overseas. But once we took them into our confidence, they were absolutely brilliant, and very, very supportive of me. We had regular phone calls from Murray's sister. We told our closest friends and they were wonderful. I had friends who rang every day to say, 'Shari, just thinking of you. Hope you're having a good day. Give me a call if there's anything I can do.' That helped a lot. The person who was essential in getting me through it all was my mother. Without her, I'm not sure how things would have gone.

In terms of Murray's work associates, the key individual was Bill

Francis at Newstalk ZB, who couldn't have been more helpful to us both. There were times when Bill and I were conversing on a daily basis, as he sought to handle the inquisitive media and Murray's work situation.

The people at Sky, whom we took into our confidence, responded marvellously because of the respect they have for Bill Francis and the relationships that had been forged with Murray. They were guided by the timeframes Bill devised. Murray's colleagues were a great support, willingly filling in for him on his television programme. Incredibly, throughout all this we didn't lose one of the programme's advertisers or sponsors, which is a mark of respect for Murray.

We're still on the journey that certainly isn't over yet. In many respects, it's similar to the one Murray and all alcoholics must take on the path to recovery — acceptance of the illness, management of the medication and fearless communication with professional medical people. We realised life would be difficult when Murray's depression struck but I don't think anyone could ever have been prepared for the chaos that engulfed us. What helped me to survive, and remains my most constant memory through it all, was Murray's courage, and the tenacity he displayed as he fought back. I look forward to the future. With Murray's courage and my support, we will finish up with an even stronger relationship.

Life without alcohol

The real test for the alcoholic is not to stop drinking but to stay stopped. I had my last drink on 14 January 1978.

My drinking story is as boring as anyone else's. Suffice to say, I'd tried everything to get my drunkenness under control: drinking at set times only, drinking only beer, drinking only spirits, not drinking for a day or a week (although never for a month). No matter what I tried, I quickly reverted to my costly old patterns.

Unquestionably, I suffered a personality change once the alcohol reached a particular level in my system. Confidence became arrogance, seriousness gave way to deep intensity and humour metamorphosed into bizarre behaviour, but most of all I wanted to fight.

Booze landed me in all sorts of trouble, costing me jobs and friends. It brought me enemies, took me to jail and court and landed me a criminal conviction for assault. Most of all, it cost me self-respect. Initially, it was the threat of losing my wife and family that led me to seek help. Like so many suffering alcoholics, I didn't know where to turn.

In my autobiography, *The Man in the Glass*, I outline the advice given to me by Owen Baragwanath and my introduction to a worldwide fellowship that's based on anonymity. The rules preclude me from associating my name with it because if I ever resort to the bottle it will degrade the fellowship. The fellowship is based on the principle of 'one day at a time'. Quite simply, you try and stay sober for 24 hours.

By the time most alcoholics arrive at the point I was then, their lives are a complete mess. They have hit rock bottom and have only three choices left: death, madness or recovery. Many either die from alcohol-related illnesses or take their own lives.

Alcoholism is a family disease. Conservatively, it's estimated that a drinking alcoholic affects 10 others. In my case, my drunkenness had an impact on many more, but it is those closest to you who get hurt the most. Looking back now, I see that my dad was the worst affected. He couldn't believe his only son was squandering opportunities that had never been given to him. My sister, to whom I'm now extremely close, used to shudder when friends asked if I was related to her.

Fortunately, when I arrived at the doors of the fellowship there were some old-timers on hand who spelt out the basics. Like most alcoholics, my greatest concern in those initial weeks was to establish whether I was an alcoholic. Why that should have been an issue is completely beyond me now. If I had really wanted proof, I could have asked anyone involved in Otago or Auckland rugby or cricket, anyone who had attended Otago University in the 1960s, Christchurch Teachers' College in 1969 or anyone who taught alongside me.

For some stupid reason the public seems to judge alcoholism in terms of quantity. How often have you heard it said: 'So and so can't be alcoholic because he only drinks on Saturday night'? It isn't the amount you drink. It's what the alcohol does to you. If it induces a personality change or causes you to behave erratically, you need help. You're an alcoholic. Instead, I was told to look for the similarities, not the differences, something that made sense to me. And I was told to extract the cotton wool from my ears and stuff it in my mouth, something I have great difficulty doing.

The similarities were immediately apparent. Most alcoholics are perfectionists who often drink out of frustration when they cannot achieve their goals. They find compromise difficult and have a low tolerance of others' foibles. Most alcoholics are highly sensitive and emotional. Over the years, I've witnessed hundreds break down while sharing their experiences. Once they have a period of sobriety behind them, their emotions strengthen and are controlled.

All alcoholics suffer from a progressive disease and all are recovering, not recovered. Even my close friends occasionally suggest I could have a quiet drink 'without becoming drunk again'. What they don't appreciate is that I'm just one drink away from becoming a drunk. If I were to put alcohol into my system, it would be as though I had been drinking right through the last 26 years. Just because you've stopped drinking doesn't mean the disease has gone away. Twenty-six years ago I was out of control and the thought of how I would react to alcohol again is frightening. I am certain that I would soon be either dead or mad.

The main reason I won't drink again is that it would mean turning my back on a programme of recovery that has turned my life around. That programme identifies in the first instance that the suffering alcoholic's life has become unmanageable and can only be brought back on track by placing belief in a higher power. That isn't to say this is a religious programme but it certainly has a strong spiritual base. It naturally follows that the recovering alcoholic then addresses problem areas, makes amends to people who have been adversely affected by their behaviour in the past and gets on with the basic business of living.

One strong proviso is that a personal inventory be taken regularly so that the recovering alcoholic is constantly evaluating their actions. Part of the obligation is to spread the message by assisting those who are suffering. In this particular area, I was a total failure! Too often I've met people who say they want to recover but really don't have the willpower to get started. When they fail after being given the message, I've been tempted to deliver the next message as a bunch of fives — not exactly a loving, caring way of helping them to recover!

However, over the past seven years I've been amazed at the number of men, literally dozens of them, who have come up to me, particularly at rugby matches, drawn me aside and said that reading my book *The Man in the Glass* has helped them 'get off the piss'.

My powerlessness over alcohol cost me a career in law, provincial status in rugby and cricket and a job at Auckland Grammar, and it was about to cost me my marriage and what I cherished most, my kids. My life had become unmanageable, and like a lot of alcoholics, I didn't trust anyone or anything. Fate intervened and I had to rush from Orewa to Dunedin because of a family tragedy. Suddenly, I was face to face with a crisis. I had nowhere to turn, nowhere to go. I dropped to my knees, and I assure you they were virgin knees, and prayed for help. It worked and I was able to cope.

We all have our unique ways of doing things and in my case they were significantly different. Most people tend to confess their mistakes to a close friend. I didn't want to inflict everything I'd been up to on anyone I knew. Instead, one wet winter afternoon I pulled into the courtyard of a Roman Catholic church and pressed the button on the confessional. Some young priest was shaken from his cloisters by a voice booming through with, 'Father, I've got plenty to say.'

The poor priest copped the lot. When I'd finished, he stammered, 'Well . . . well . . . I . . .'

'Father, you don't have to say anything. I had to share my story with another human being and I've just done that, so, see ya!' And I left the confessional, leaving behind one extremely confused young priest.

Sober alcoholics favour finality and conclusion and cope badly with anything that's hanging over, if you'll pardon the pun. I knew I had to prioritise my life. And top of the list was dealing with anything that jeopardised my sobriety because if I lost that then I would have nothing.

My priorities are my sobriety, my family and my work. They can always get another broadcaster. There's a queue out there waiting for me to topple off my perch and I know, especially in broadcasting, that if they can get someone as good but cheaper, they'll take him. Family is different, and mine stuck by me.

I've learned never to head for bed with the day's events on my mind, and I also try never to handle the same piece of paper twice. I rarely change my mind once I've made a decision and I try not to have regrets.

I've been told that 'yesterday is history, tomorrow is mystery'. Recovering alcoholics live for today only. Once you've made amends there's nothing you can do about yesterday, and as for tomorrow, who knows what's in store? Living one day at a time, as though it's your last, makes every happening, every person you encounter and everything you do extremely special.

I learned that I mustn't get too tired, too hungry or too thirsty. Whenever I hear Sir Bob Charles talk about the routine he has followed so closely to ensure his extraordinary near 50-year survival on the professional golf circuit I think about this advice. Bob follows a strict diet that includes a kiwifruit a day. And Dave Stockton, that fine American golfer who played so much of the circuit with Bob, says that if you're having dinner with the knight, it will be an early night because Bob's always in bed by 9.30 p.m. I hate late nights and can't stand it if I'm listening to someone half lubricated droning on after ten o'clock. To put it simply, I had to learn a whole new blueprint for living. This wasn't easy for me in the early days because so much of my life was centred on local pubs. Shortly after shifting back to Auckland I was given a reminder of this.

I was selling cricket gear at the time and a prospective client wanted to meet me at the Masonic Hotel in Devonport. It was dreadfully hot, humid Auckland afternoon and when I arrived I was asked what I wanted to drink. When I nominated an orange juice, the guy went up to the bar and returned to our table with a glass of orange and a jug of beer. When it was my turn to shout, I brought back a jug of orange juice and a glass of beer. He got the message.

The story highlights the attitude of most people to non-drinkers. They think we're different — from Mars, if you like — and that they're entitled to consume greater quantities of alcohol than we are of non-alcoholic drinks. If my wife Sharon and I split the bill with the rest of the table after dining out, no one ever suggests we shouldn't be contributing to their expensive wine. I'm not complaining; it's a small price to pay. And we have all varieties of alcohol in our own house because I don't want my non-drinking to affect other people's lives the way my drinking did.

I'm often asked how I cope in the sporting scene where so much alcohol is consumed. To me, it's a non-issue. Usually, I'm working while they're drinking and most are so keen on topping themselves up they don't notice that one person is abstaining.

Most people are able to drink socially but 10 per cent are like me. Do the mathematics and you get some idea of the chronic alcoholism that grips our nation. And I'm cynical enough to believe that no political party wants to address this question. Too many of our leaders have had obvious problems with the booze and the amount of tax from alcohol that goes into the government's coffers helps to keep the country afloat. Some of my friends go further and suggest the government would be frightened of a sober society's interpretation of what it was up to!

Certainly, my experience as chief executive and founder of the Foundation for Alcohol and Drug Education (FADE) has highlighted the unwillingness of both the Labour and National parties to do anything meaningful in drug and alcohol education. During a four-year period we made 13 trips to Parliament seeking support but all we received were broken promises. I'm convinced that not one recent New Zealand politician has given a stuff about teenage drug and alcohol abuse. I used to say that the only time we would get action was when a senior Cabinet minister's son or daughter suicided as a result of abuse, but that has already happened and no one took up the cause.

I'm often approached by people who have a family member or close friend with alcohol problems. My response is always the same: 'Get them to ring me if they want help'. In 90 per cent of the cases I never hear from them again. It doesn't matter how much someone else wants to assist, if the alcoholic doesn't seek help there's no way he or she will get better. The alcoholic must want to get sober, and must want that more than anything else in the world.

Coupled with that, the alcoholic must be prepared to go to any lengths to become sober. Only complete dedication will lead to eventual sobriety.

There's no question that the sober alcoholics who get five-star sobriety have a strong spiritual base. They may not be religious, and in fact most aren't, but they do believe that a power greater than themselves will restore their sanity. When I face a problem over 6ft 3in (my height) I hand it over to my God. Initially, I used to take it back because I thought he might stuff it up. I still figure that with all these alkies asking for his help, he's so busy that I'm best to give it a shot first.

One statement that's had a lasting impact on me came from an old-timer at a critical time in my journey to sobriety. I'd just missed out on the headmaster's appointment at Takapuna Grammar (after seven years as the deputy principal) and my first wife was dying of cancer. The old-timer listened to my woes and suggested that if everyone was asked to put their problems on the table at the start of the evening, at the end they would go to the table, pick up their own problems and go home with them. His message was that we were the ones best equipped to deal with our own problems.

I'm not saying that this is the only way of staying 'stopped' but it's the only way I know. If people find me blunt, direct, straight and honest, it's because those qualities are the basis of the programme that was shared with me. There's no room for bullshit and most sober alcoholics are equipped with a built-in bullshit detector.

My daily focus, my prioritising, my in-your-face attitude and my sense of humour are all a direct result of watching and learning from the old-timers. Wherever I go I run into people with whom I have a special bond. It's a bit like a secret society. They only need to tell me they 'belong' and I know where they've been and they know where I've been.

Unquestionably, getting sober is the most important thing in my life. Staying sober remains a daily challenge. Many of my close friends thought I would drink again during my depression in 2003. Frankly, I would have preferred to kill myself than drink again and go through that hell I experienced. I want to die sober and if I follow a few simple principles, I will.

I'm not good at praying, but one prayer I use is: 'God grant me the serenity to accept the things I cannot change, courage to change the things I can and the wisdom to know the difference.'

Talkback callers

The major mistake most talkback hosts make is to think it's talk-at, not talkback. The major mistake most critics make is to take it seriously, when most of it's just a safety valve.

Talkback is as old as civilisation: one of Rome's techniques for keeping citizens happy was the forum, where citizens could air their views, voice their complaints, discuss the issues of the day, have their gripe without anyone taking them too seriously. It also served as a gauge for those in power to find out what the public was thinking. Nothing has changed, except now it's on radio and the audience is wider.

Talkback rates. When 1ZB took the major punt and became Newstalk ZB, its ratings dropped away disastrously. People were used to the mix of music, news and light comment championed by Merv Smith. Then suddenly, Paul Holmes, a Wellingtonian, started to push his opinions, views and philosophy. They turned off in thousands. But the management stuck to its guns and slowly the tide turned. Newstalk ZB has dominated the Auckland ratings for the past 14 years.

Why do people listen to talkback? It has an element of unpredictability that's exciting. You know what to expect for the next couple of minutes if Glen Campbell breaks into 'Galveston', but if Leighton Smith asks, 'Is Helen Clark doing a good job?' anything can happen. Talkback can be controversial, almost defamatory at times, and people love that. It's often confrontational — the best issues are those that split the public down the middle.

The best hosts are highly opinionated and prepared to stick to their argument even if public opinion starts to run against them. In this regard, Leighton Smith is the best in the business. Often arrogant, always opinionated, usually logical, he espouses his views with papal certainty.

Talkback can be fun and highly entertaining. When Martin Devlin is out of control, I'm glued to the radio, not knowing what's going to happen next; usually, Marty hasn't got a clue either. He can be hilarious, right over top and completely wrong, but it's great radio. The man's an entertainer. When he first burst on to the scene, a number of people said, 'How do you feel about Devlin challenging you?' I never saw it that way. In his outrageous way Martin gets away with things that I wouldn't dare attempt. Conversely, Martin couldn't do what I do. We're complementary. I listen to his show because we're so different.

Talkback rates because it's current, frequently a knee-jerk reaction to the news at the top of the hour. Callers often grab the phone before they've thought the issue through, but it remains a gut-level reaction, something you're not going to get in a newspaper column written hours after the event by a journalist who's had time to weigh up both sides of the argument.

Talkback is often raw emotion based on subjectivity. Callers speak from the heart, not the head. Most ring in because they have a gripe and the only way they can release their frustration is to air their views. Often they're over the top, completely out of control, furious at an issue or individual and don't care what they say. This is the most anxious time for the host because he sits right on the edge of a defamation action. If a caller defames someone, the radio station can be guilty also, because it has provided the medium for the defamation.

Talkback succeeds because it's on the edge — of defamation, of emotions, of objectivity. Consequently, hosting a programme is like living on the edge, something a print or television journalist would never experience. The talkback host spends his entire shift making instant judgments and the best he can hope for is to get most of them right. It's a draining, emotionally taxing, exhausting business that leaves little room for error. People tune into talkback because they can hear a cross-section of society, much more so than from reading the letters to the editor in their local newspaper. In their normal lives, they're never likely to have any contact with many of the people they're listening to. For some, talkback is like an audio *Coronation Street* or *Days of Our Lives*, a continuing and current soap opera. Most people listen because they love gossip and talkback is full of gossip. Some of the big stories of New Zealand sport have been blown on talkback.

A Wellington taxi driver informed the nation that he had picked up Chris Cairns at 4 a.m. from a flat to take him to the hotel where the New Zealand cricketers were staying. It was right in the middle of a test match and callers reacted instantly. New Zealand Cricket tried to cover up but only made matters worse.

The morning of the announcement of Graham Henry as All Black coach, a carpet layer in Christchurch rang through with the news that he was working in the house of a current All Black who had been told John Mitchell was dropped. Both stories highlight that we're just a village and the town crier is radio talkback.

What do you need to be a talkback host? The most important quality is to be a good listener. The truism 'God gave you two ears and one mouth and God isn't stupid' applies here more than in any other job. The public doesn't want to hear the same voice droning on monotonously, hour after hour. Nor will it listen to someone who's always right and never acknowledges when he or she is wrong.

The public is actually most forgiving of hosts who make mistakes, identifying them more as friends who got it wrong rather than as journalists who are always expected to be accurate because they have time to substantiate their facts and figures. A talkback host who isn't opinionated isn't worth listening to. The public expects you to take stands and to be consistent in your views. Middle ground is grey, boring, dull and an immediate turn-off. At times you find yourself out on a limb, without friends for support. That's the time to hang in there.

An ego is vital in this business. All the good broadcasters possess a well-developed one and, frankly, if you didn't have a healthy ego you wouldn't be capable of turning on the microphone. It's your egotism that leads you to tell callers what you think about the issue. In reality, most of them don't care what you think. They've telephoned to put you right, to promote their opinion and they rarely hear your side of the argument.

You need a thick skin to survive in talkback. I believe I operate on about a 60 per cent approval rating. Consequently, at any given time, 40 per cent of listeners are thinking, 'Deaker, you're a bloody idiot' or 'Who does he think he is?' You must accept, too, that other journalists will treat you with disdain. This is because you earn four or five times more than most of them, for what they regard as flaky work. If the talkback-host role is as simple as some have suggested, it's surprising more of them haven't sought to involve themselves in it.

The biggest barrel I ever copped was in the Eden Park car park following an Auckland rugby game. Mark Carter, the Auckland flanker, was an All Black at the time, and his selection had been severely criticised by callers, particularly those living in the Canterbury region. Leaving a rugby ground two hours after the final whistle is always hazardous because most of the patrons still there have seriously overimbibed. This particular night I was accosted by a middle-aged woman brandishing a glass of wine.

'Why are you crucifying my son?' she asked.

'Lady, I don't even know who you are,' I replied.

'I'm Mark Carter's mother and I cannot believe . . .' And away she went, launching into a most remarkable tirade against talkback host Deaker. It would have been a pointless exercise to try convincing her that I'd been more supportive of her son's play than anyone else on air. I just stood there and took the flak while onlookers tried to decide whether this was part of the paid entertainment.

Talkback hosts need to know when they've gone too far. Shortly after Possum Bourne was killed, I learned that there was much more to the accident than the authorities were letting on. I raised it on the night he was buried and was rightly taken to task by my first two callers. I immediately backed off and acknowledged that I was out of order.

You need a sense of humour to succeed in talkback; particularly, you need to be able to laugh at yourself. I'm not good at predicting results, although I did select South Africa to win the 1995 World Cup and England to succeed in 2003. In between, I've got too many wrong and Willie Jackson, the former MP and a part-time broadcaster himself, once rang in protesting that I'd nominated the Kiwi league team to win, complaining he'd just backed them. Now that I was picking them they were bound to lose, he said. What else could you do except laugh?

A talkback host needs to be consistent, always up, focused, sharp and on the edge. Most people listen for only three to five minutes at any one time, often while they're driving to the supermarket. Certainly, Auckland's traffic problems are one of the keys to Newstalk ZB's success. Many of our listeners are tuned into car radios during peak-hour traffic. For the midweek evening show a lot of the callers are men travelling home from work who will take in from 10 to 30 minutes of the programme. Many of them tune into the show halfway through, so it's vital that I periodically provide a precis of the opening interview and the subsequent line of discussion.

During the weekends, many listeners obviously have my programme on in the background while they go about their household chores, be it dishwashing, painting or gardening. Consequently, the programme has to be a sequence of self-contained segments that are seamless — not an easy task.

To maintain the required energy levels for my six-hour shifts on Saturday and Sunday, I'm constantly snacking on bananas, sandwiches or small cakes. I try to avoid coffee because it hypes me up excessively but I drink water or tea all the time. The only breaks you get during a six-hour shift are at the top of the hour, and they're so short that by the time you've been to the toilet and made a cup of tea, you're straight back on air. Ninety-eight per cent of the programme is live so you must concentrate fully for the whole time. The first three hours are reasonably comfortable but real discipline is required for the second half. Broadcasters have to be careful to avoid coughs, colds and stomach upsets. Being physically and mentally attuned is absolutely imperative. It concerns me that there are few aged broadcasters around. Most don't seem to make old bones.

My father, who was an outstanding teacher and headmaster, said he knew he'd done a top job if at the end of his teaching day he felt like a worn-out rag. When I come off the air, I have nothing left. At times, it's frightening. The lift at the Radio Network offices in central Auckland occasionally breaks down. When I finish at six o'clock on a Sunday, I pray it will still be operating, because I often feel I'll be incapable of walking down the three flights of stairs. I rarely venture out on Friday or Saturday nights and never on Sunday evenings. It usually takes me until the following Wednesday before I'm fully energised again, particularly with my Monday night TV show dropped in for good measure.

All broadcasters must be able to communicate with their audience. The moment they fail to achieve this, they may as well turn the microphone off. There are no benefits in being excessively intellectual, academic or smart. While you're directing your comments to Mr and Mrs Average you must also try to interest those at extreme ends of the intellectual spectrum. It's not so much how you say it as what you say.

I've spent a lifetime watching people trying to get their message across and those who fail most often are those who try to be too clever. Teachers and university lecturers often make the mistake of believing that communication is about impressing their audience. It isn't. It's about getting your message across.

You need to respect your callers, not upset them. Just because someone doesn't agree with you, or can't get their tenses correct, or drops in the odd 'aah' or 'um' is no cause for you to belittle them. Without callers, you're simply not going to survive. They've taken the time to ring you; the least you can do is listen to them. In this respect, I find Darcy Waldegrave and Graham Hill, two relatively new hosts to Radio Sport, to be right on the money.

Most listeners can tell from the tone of your voice whether you're genuine and honest. They want to hear their talkback hosts giving an honest opinion in a direct manner and it doesn't worry them if they disagree with the statements made and conclusions reached. All the better if they do, because then they're likely to call in and put the broadcaster right.

You need to be provocative, able to identify the issue and then take a stand on it. I've never been so far from general opinion as I was with the sub-hosting of the Rugby World Cup. Even before the announcement that we had lost the rights, I was levelling blame at the NZRU but this was an unpopular stance because the knee-jerk public reaction was to blame O'Neill and the Aussies for doing the dirty on us. That feeling was accentuated by Andy Haden, who suggested O'Neill and Vernon Pugh were in cohorts, further claiming they were supported by 'that idiot Deaker'. I made the mistake of taking a cheap shot at Andy, declaring I had two degrees and a diploma while I couldn't remember him ever finishing anything at university. Although true, this was completely irrelevant.

Talkback caller Alan rang up and rubbished me for being disloyal and ill-informed. Within three weeks the tide had turned and the same man rang to apologise. His behaviour is typical of most callers who are genuine, honest Kiwis, prepared to acknowledge mistakes. It's a shame some talkback hosts aren't as forthcoming.

Any talkback host worth his salt knows his audience and knows what will make them react. Unquestionably, the best talkback topic of my time was the John Hart–Laurie Mains debate. It split the country evenly and set north against south, urban against rural, the new corporates against the old grass roots. I milked it until it was dry.

In more recent times the debate over the defectors from Team New Zealand was just as lively. My position was clear from the outset and has never changed. What did surprise me was the level of support for Coutts, Butterworth, Daubney, Jones and Phipps. The John Mitchell–Graham Henry debate never really got under way because Henry refused to comment publicly while Mitchell embarked on a presidential campaign, suddenly available to the media he had neglected for two years.

Year after year the Halberg Awards provoke prolonged debate, mainly because of the hopelessly flawed judging system that compares apples with oranges, teams with individuals, women with men. And too often the judges get it wrong. Their worst decision was the refusal to grant Blyth Tait, the equestrian champion, the supreme award after he won everything — Badminton, Burleigh and the world crown. If he'd been allocated a rocking horse, he would still have come in first. Instead, the panel opted for Rob Waddell, a champion for sure, but one who that year achieved only a fraction of what Tait did. The public quickly assessed that other factors came into the panel's decision and roasted them unmercifully. It was already clear that rowing and rowers were the favourites with the selection panel, and talkback callers were loud in their criticism.

Why would anyone want to ring a talkback host? Some are negative and have a particular bitch: they have something to say and nothing is going to stop them. On a number of occasions I've tried to introduce them by saying, 'What did you think of what Bill just said?' But they can't comment because they didn't hear a word Bill said and they're not likely to hear one thing I say. These single-purpose callers are the worst. They rarely contribute to the discussion and are never willing to compromise.

Some callers telephone out of total frustration, seeing talkback as the only place where they can voice an opinion. Although often angry initially, many of these callers can listen and debate an issue. Some are prepared to change their stance if suddenly confronted with a fresh set of facts.

Others call because they want to catch you out. They usually start with, 'Do you recall me ringing you three months ago?' Yeah, right. I sometimes field more than 90 calls a weekend, so the chances are remote that I'll remember a caller that far back, even if events in the meantime have proved them right.

Some have agendas. Most of Canterbury seems to have a common one: to see 15 red and blacks in the All Blacks. One caller, Peter, took to faxing me daily, suggesting I was often one-eyed and vindictive towards the red and blacks. They really are a race apart. I discovered how passionate they were when I criticised the Cantabs for booing Adam Parore while he was playing for New Zealand at Lancaster Park (before it became Jade Stadium, I think). At that time, the Cantabs wanted Lee Germon to be the keeper. A couple of days after I'd ripped into them, this letter arrived:

> Deaker, you dork. You talk so much shit. To say that little Adam got a raw deal is like suggesting Helen Clark is sexy. If you think he got shit, wait until you see what you get when you come down here, you bloody dork.
>
> You Dorklanders are all the same, all grease and Brylcreem, white shoes and gold chains. It's our ground and we'll boo the little shit as much as we like. Duck waddle walk, greasy hair, stupid smirk and can't bat for shit.
>
> And as for criticising us Cantabs, why, we hold the Ranfurly Shield, the Super 12, the women's cricket title and the men's cricket title.
>
> The only competition you Aucklanders are likely to win is a wanking contest and I suggest you and little Adam get out the front.
> Yours, Bill Thompson

The most useful Canterbury correspondent or talkback caller I have is a bloke who calls himself Chris Clarke. An ardent league man who has written to me over a 10-year period espousing the virtues of league and decrying rugby, he's extremely knowledgeable and for a time I thought it was the league writer, John Coffey, operating under a pseudonym. Clarke's chief argument is that the rugby establishment is braindead and all the recent innovations made have been flogged from league. He once listed 15 so-called innovations such as a video referee, talking flags, timekeepers, names on jerseys and yellow and red cards as ideas that originated in league. It is the arrogance of rugby's establishment that upsets him the most and he's scathing in his criticism of the 'ra-ra' game. The vitriol is always penned in beautiful handwriting and the ideas are expressed with clarity and succinctness.

First-time callers are always refreshing and different. Many of them are nervous, but it's important to nurture them because, given confidence, they can bring variety to the programme. Most of them haven't rung before because they've never been targeted or they simply haven't been able to get through.

The regulars vary from your bread-and-butter types to the utter pains in the arse. Some believe they're more important than the host and turn listeners off. Worse, some of the regulars, talkback addicts, are on the phone to all the ZB hosts, all the Radio Sport hosts and through to Radio Pacific as well. These professional callers, on ego trips, invariably speak with authority and decisiveness. They're to be avoided at all costs.

Yet other regulars can make your show. 'Mark' has been a regular caller on league and cricket for a decade. He's provocative, at times scathingly so, and scornful of the establishment but generally on the money. The Mad Butcher hates him and is always going on about 'that bloody Mark' whom he believes has never done anything for league. I gave 'Mark' a prize once, solely to help identify him. Immediately, the Butcher was on the attack. 'That Mark hasn't even got the guts to go by his real name,' the Butcher thundered. Quick as a flash, 'Mark' was on the line and giving his real name as Zane. He copped a fair bit of flak from callers: one asked, 'Why listen to that Mark or Zane when he obviously doesn't even know who he is?' But 'Mark' kept bouncing back, and continues to contribute positively to the show.

The best talkback caller on rugby is a former club coach from the Wairarapa, Jim Burke, who is knowledgeable, astute, sound and earthy. He pays me the compliment of not ringing anyone else. Jim has extraordinary foresight and is the best picker of results I've come across. For example, after I'd rubbished Auckland following its loss to Bay of Plenty in 2003, when it seemed Wayne Pivac's team could miss the play-offs, Jim rang through with the prediction that Auckland would win the Air New Zealand NPC and pick up the Ranfurly Shield. It did. He also nominated an Australia–England final to the 2003 World Cup, with England to win.

Jim and I have been the most vociferous critics of current All Black forward play and between us we conjured up the term the 'front few', as opposed to the tight five. We're also in sync about the need for a top goalkicker, averaging at least close to an 80 per cent strike rate. I look forward to his calls because what he has to say will inevitably be basic, yet different.

'McLean' is the pseudonym for Murray Lane, a bloke in his sixties who lives in Christchurch but who can identify other colours besides red and black. His major beef is the quality of passing in rugby and he's justifiably confused by the inability of backs to put the pass in front of the player running onto it. He hates flat backlines and was after Graham Henry at the first opportunity to check how deep he intended to stand his backs.

There's an Auckland fanatic who goes to Eden Park attired in an Auckland jersey emblazoned with the legend 'Mrs Spencer' and a blue wig. She has a voice like a rasp which she sometimes shares with the nation after an Auckland victory by singing, 'We are blue, we are white, we are Auckland dynamite.' I shudder as I contemplate the number of Canterbury listeners turning off. Pete the Urban Maori is the most unusual caller I tolerate. At times he's so remote you'd think he was ringing in from Mars. He speaks a version of James Joyce's stream of consciousness, but occasionally drops in an absolute pearl, as when he claimed the All Blacks' inability to win the big ones was a direct result of an education system that encourages mediocrity. Pete carried it a bit far when he further suggested today's youth are so confused they probably think second is better than first because it's twice as many!

Kelvin of Hamilton is crazy about women's sport, particularly netball. He rings up in the middle of a debate on the Rugby World Cup with this opening comment: 'I want to talk about some real world champions.' He watches every netball game going. Since Mystery Creek became a major venue for the game, Kelvin has been in his element. We don't receive many calls from the Waikato and Kelvin has almost become the voice of Mooloo.

Steve Harris is a Ngapuhi from Whangarei who has been living in west Auckland for some years, although he still supports the Cambridge Blues. A rep for Coca-Cola, he's constantly tuned to Radio Sport. Until recently, his sole topic of conversation was rugby but professionalism and his proximity to the All Blacks via his job has put him off. Now he's just as likely to ring up about outrigger canoeing, a sport in which his family is fully involved. Coke is one of the companies that was disillusioned by the current All Blacks' attitude. A few years ago, Coke turned on a function and all the All Blacks mixed in. In 2003, when a similar event was arranged, the All Blacks and their management preferred to keep to themselves.

Murray Brooks is responsible for giving underwater hockey a profile envied by sports with many more competitors. Murray rings up from tournaments all around the country with the latest results. He makes it sound as exciting as Murray Walker calling a Formula One race or Winston McCarthy commentating the fourth test between the All Blacks and the Springboks in 1956. A CNN news reporter was in New Zealand and heard Murray in full cry on my show. As a result the network sent a crew to New Zealand to film a game of underwater hockey. The mind boggles at the number of viewers that feature would have reached.

Gregory Fortuin, the former race relations conciliator, and I didn't get off to a great start. I forget the details but Gregory felt that my stance on something to do with South Africa bordered on racism. I held my ground and a lively discussion ensued. Gregory loves to debate and remains a passionate supporter of the Springboks while committed to the Kiwis in everything else. It's a strange stance, given that the Springboks were one of the final bastions of apartheid.

Another regular is a bloke called Trevor, who just happens to be Trevor Mallard, the Minister of Sport. At times he can't help himself. Something I say provokes him and he's on the line. I don't always recognise his voice but he invariably has a contribution worth listening to.

Sir Howard Morrison sometimes calls in. Howard's grievance is that today's youth aren't disciplined enough. To be more precise, he's highly critical of their lack of self-discipline and their inability to push themselves to the limit. He's an advocate of competition, of acknowledging winners.

Jock is a caller from Dunedin who constantly despairs of the Highlanders and Otago rugby. During the Laurie Mains–John Hornbrook fiasco, Jock almost had apoplexy over the treatment Laurie was receiving. When the NZRU settled out of court, Jock was totally vindicated.

The most difficult regular caller is John from Invercargill. He has often gleaned information that borders on the defamatory and although he speaks in Southland gibberish, I remain poised on the cut-off button throughout his call. It usually takes him some time to get to the point because he fancies himself as an agrarian philosopher.

The best technique with talkback is to turn the callers over reasonably quickly. If they haven't made their point within two minutes, they're unlikely to have one. The real trick is to discard useless calls quickly and milk the good ones. It's important to let people with a contrary view to your own have their say so that the programme is balanced. You don't have to agree with them and, in fact, you'd be unwise to do so, but it's essential they be heard.

There's nothing worse on radio that having two people speaking at the same time. I avoid that by putting the caller on hold while I make my point, reintroducing them once I've finished.

Greg Billings, my producer, screens all the calls and over 14 years he has become expert at it. During the commercial break he identifies the next four callers for me: 'Kelvin the netball nutter on one, stupid Dave on two, Sue on three, she may have a point, and John on four, be bloody careful with him'.

The worst time for talkback is between 5 p.m. and 6 p.m. on Sunday evening. It's the end of the weekend and those without families or separated from them have had a miserable day and many of them have tried to drown their sorrows. Their only contact with the outside world has been via talkback radio and so many are full of poison, and alcohol, when they ring in.

By 5.45 p.m. on one particular bad Sunday, Greg had screened out 90 per cent of the callers and I was screaming down the intercom to him, 'Who's next?' Radio Sport was off the air and some kid fresh out of broadcasting school couldn't get it back on, some clown was trying to claim a prize by ringing the front door bell and Greg's horse had just finished last at Ellerslie. It all proved too much for him. He stood up and exploded with, 'I'm surrounded by fuckwits!'

Sadly, too many boring people get to air. To some extent, this is a direct result of the current excess of talkback on the New Zealand airwaves. In sport, particularly, we're now forced to listen to some people pushing their particular bandwagon from host to host. This can be controlled only if hosts refuse to give airtime to habitual callers, if producers are particularly vigilant and if hosts encourage first-time callers.

In general, talkback is fun, challenging, entertaining and, most of all, unpredictable. It's the biggest class I've ever taught and certainly the one with the largest range of intellect. You can go from a complete moron to an expert in a second. And all the time you're on the edge.

Regulars on the show

Gordon Bray has been my Australian correspondent from the time I started with Newstalk ZB. He epitomises professionalism, diligence and reliability. Gordon never lets you down. And he has been invaluable in opening doors to the Australian sporting elite. Mention of Gordon's name and his relationship to me and the Australian sporting stars relax and talk. They recognise that he's a man of integrity with a real love of sport and a passion for rugby in particular. One-eyed first for Australia and second for New South Wales, he's as much a part of the Australian sporting scene as George Gregan, Andrew Johns and Steve Waugh.

In 2003, Gordon was unnecessarily put through the mill. A new boss at Channel Seven decided he wanted a more controversial caller and Gordon was forced to share the early rounds of the World Cup with another commentator. There was no comparison. Gordon was clearly superior. John O'Neill expressed his unhappiness to me and vowed to contact Channel Seven on Gordon's behalf. I couldn't see Chris Moller doing the same for me.

Sandy Myhre is an outstanding journalist in a motor world dominated by males. Her skill, expertise and, above all, her determination identify her as someone special, so special, in fact, that even the most chauvinistic motor lord accepts that Sandy knows what makes cars go fast. More than that, she has a particular knack of hunting out the interesting details, those aspects of the sport that interest not only the petrol-heads but also fascinate those of us with only dashboard knowledge. A measure of her professionalism was conveyed to me when, 11 years ago, she reported to us from the track following the death of the former world champion Denny Hulme. What I didn't know at that time was that Sandy was Hulme's partner. It must have been a harrowing experience for her. Sandy's book *Fifty Years of New Zealand Motor Sport* is an absolute classic, written with an eye for detail and containing a large amount of previously untold information. Above all this, Sandy brings a woman's perspective to sport, something that is all too often overlooked.

Ron Barr, our regular from San Francisco, is opinionated, authoritative and brimming with confidence and information. Most correspondents need to be fed six or seven questions to help them through their slot, but one or two is all it takes to get Ron rolling. Who and what he doesn't know regarding American sport isn't worth knowing. When he doesn't know something, he makes it up, and it sounds even better. I suspect he isn't the 'authority' he would have us believe, but that doesn't decrease the interest and intensity he brings to his reports. Ron can speak on anything. At the height of the debate on why the All Blacks lost five in a row, I concluded my interview with him by saying, 'Well, Ron, you're a refreshing change from debating the All Blacks' failure.'

Quick as a flash he responded with, 'While on that subject, Murray, I want to point out that . . .' And for five minutes he proceeded to string together all the clichés he'd listened to over a couple of decades accounting for why the San Francisco 49ers had lost a game. It was an amazing performance. Two completely different sports but just by substituting the name 49ers for All Blacks he covered every excuse my callers had come up with over the preceding couple of weeks.

It was Ron more than anyone who gave me the confidence to become more entrepreneurial as a journalist, to care for sponsors and to be commercially astute. In the tough capitalistic world of American sports journalism you can never forget the hand that feeds you. Ron suggested to me that I 'sell Murray Deaker'. Hence, *Deaker on Sport* became Murray and Sharon's commercial enterprise, marketed in association with Sky Television. We owned the commercial content immediately before and after the programme plus the segments within. Sharon sold the advertisements as well as the sponsored segments. She did such a fine job of looking after the sponsors that she eventually did herself out of a job. Ron also helped me to overcome my fear of modern technology. I'm computer illiterate: I wrote this book by hand. I feared that modern technology would overtake me and render me obsolete. Ron wouldn't have a Barr of that. He stressed that 'content is king' and a bloke like me is pure gold in this modern technological age. It might have been American bull, but Ron is convincing and I bought into it.

The Minstrel has become a major component of my radio show. Every Saturday around 12.50 p.m. Mark de Lacy lets rip, in his own inimitable style, in verse or song, at the main talking point from the week's sporting events. He writes his ditties the morning of the show and many of them hit the target. For many years Mark was one of the country's top bowlers and he brings to the show the view of the average Kiwi sports fan. But that's the only average thing about the Minstrel. His weekly performances are always entertaining and sometimes truly brilliant. My two favourites are:

HERE'S WHAT I TOLD MARLENE

Well, I popped into the Waipu pub just south of Whangarei;
Thought I might down a beer or three and watch the Black Caps
    play.
This old bloke with a walrus mo, a little bit pissed but keen,
Tapped the Minstrel on the shoulder and said, 'You know what I
    told Marlene?'

I said, 'What's that, mate, the test she's gone,
If you think she's not, you're off your scone.
You just can't get 500 plus — the Poms got this one over us.'
The old bloke grinned and said, 'No way, mate, we're only six down,
    it's never too late
She's all on now, they've set the scene. Here's what I told Marlene:

You've gotta have faith in Nathan 'cos he's our favourite son;
You've gotta have faith in Nathan, yeah, he's a cricketing gun;
You gotta have faith in Nathan when a testy target calls,
You gotta have faith in Nathan 'cos Astle's got the balls.'

Well, the very next indication that the old bloke might be right
Was the look I took from Nasser's face — talk about uptight.

He said, 'Oh what fun, he's got another run. Well done, son, you got
one ton.'

Well, schick bricks and pick-up sticks, no nicks, no wicks, just another bloody six.

Come on, Caddick, you're bowling like a haddock;

For God sake, Andrew, keep him in the paddock, don't panic;

Yeah, a six off his shoulder, a six off his hip,

I dunno how he hit the beauty backward over slip.

Three little ducks, that's two two two and Hoggard got one for one
four two;

A new world record for a double ton off one fifty-three, that's awe-
some, son;

If it ever gets beat Attila was a nun, a bit more help I think we would
have won.

I'll never forget what I saw that day and I won't until the day I'm
dead;

I won't forget my visit to the Waipu pub or what the old bloke said;

I'll never forget that Astle knock, it's the best that's ever been seen;

And you can bet I'll never forget what the old bloke told Marlene.

SIR PETER BLAKE

I was singing to the kids in a primary school at Halcombe yesterday;

It's a small rural community, Deaks, down Rangitikei way;

Some of the kids had red socks on, some found it difficult to laugh;

And the reason became more apparent on talking to the kids and
the staff.

It appears Halcombe School was fundraising, getting money to build
a fine hall;

Some bright spark suggested a dinner with a guest speaker. 'Who
could we call?'

How 'bout Sir Peter Blake, do you think that he might?

How much would he charge, would a grand be all right?

The principal suggested his schedule'd be tight,
But we'd write him a letter, fly them a kite.

A couple of weeks later the telephone rings;
The principal answers, he's the jack of all things.
'It's Peter Blake here, got your letter,' he said,
'I'd be delighted to do it, hope you've got a long bed.
If you pay for me petrol I'll charge you no fee.
Halcombe sounds like fun, so I'll do it for free.'
Sir Peter, the kids tell me, is incredibly cool;
You should've seen what he's wearing on visiting their school;
T-shirt and shorts and a shabby sandshoe, kinda look khaki, used to
    be blue.

The next night at the dinner, a spectacular show
Sir Peter immaculate in dark tuxedo;
But as a mark of the man, Deaks, I swear that it's true
Underneath the dress suit was the shabby sandshoe.
Eleven thousand dollars they raised for the hall
And the Halcombe community had an absolute ball.

A great kauri's been cut down in such a cruel way;
New Zealand is hurting but I know what he'd say:
Keep loyal, keep caring and stick to your gun,
And nothing's worth fighting for unless you have fun.

When the Minstrel first joined the show he was little known out-side of a group of fellow bowlers who used to giggle their heads off at his antics over a few beers at the conclusion of bowling tournaments. He's never been paid for his efforts on ZB, being quite content to merely put his phone number across with the comment, 'The Minstrel is avail-able for any party or function you may be having.'

It's worked for him. The Minstrel is now probably the highest-paid singer in New Zealand. This year he will sing in more than 250 New Zealand schools and perform at more than 30 functions. He has be-come the travelling Minstrel: he's sold his house and is permanently on the road. Everything Mark takes on he does with enthusiasm, hu-mour and no small degree of skill. With his wife, Chris, he travels throughout the country in a small truck and caravan, pursuing his two passions, singing and kite fishing. (He's constantly telling me to feature this or that kite-fishing contest on my programme.)

The Minstrel's variety and humour have made him a star of our Saturday show. While he continues to churn out the good stuff, week after week, he'll remain one of the cornerstones of the programme and, of course, the fact he doesn't want to be paid especially endears him to management.

Over the years I've developed a working relationship with a number of experts to whom I go for opinions on set topics. One of these is Ian Borthwick. He grew up in Christchurch but for the past 30 years has lived in France where he has carved out a niche for himself writing about rugby, particularly All Black rugby, for the all-sport newspaper *L'Equipe*. Most of his articles are feature-length and over the years Ian has developed relationships with some All Blacks that those of us closer to home haven't been able to match. His features on Jonah Lomu have been true exclusives and often bring to light aspects only touched on by our media.

When Ian last wrote, and spoke, about Jonah he did so fully informed by a panel of world authorities he had consulted regarding Jonah's kidney illness. Through his efforts we were finally able to understand the real battle Jonah had not only to play rugby but also to get out of bed each day and walk.

Like Gordon Bray, Ian is totally professional and hard-working yet more direct. Although he retains his affiliation with the country of his birth, he has become totally disillusioned with the All Black set-up. This reached crisis point during the 1999 World Cup campaign when *L'Equipe* had assigned Ian, for obvious reasons, to the All Blacks. He was one of 12 rugby journalists covering the tournament for the paper. When he contrasted the way he was being treated by the All Blacks with the cooperation his colleagues were receiving from other teams, Ian blew his top. He was particularly scathing of John Hart — the 'ultimate bullshitter'. He predicted that Hart's control methods and his determination to focus everything on himself would ultimately lead to the All Blacks' downfall.

On air, he told me the All Blacks were the worst communicators at the tournament, behaving in a way that wouldn't be tolerated by any other country. After the French knocked the All Blacks out of the tournament at the semifinal stage, Ian was reassigned to the Wallabies. When I met him a week later in Cardiff he was a changed man: he had a huge grin on his face and was thoroughly enjoying the World Cup.

He had arrived at the Wallabies' hotel downcast and dejected. When he walked into the bar on the Monday night, he was spotted by Tim Horan who yelled out, 'What's wrong with you, Ian? Get your arse over here and have a few beers with us.' For Ian, the contrast could not have been more profound: on the one hand, a morose, unhappy All Black camp where an international journalist found it impossible to communicate; on the other, an energetic, bright, cooperative group of Aussies prepared to talk, on the record, to a journo without an official press officer hovering.

Peter FitzSimons is the author of the best rugby book I've read. In *The Rugby Wars*, Fitzy really got to grips with the battle between RWC Ltd and the establishment, which was effectively Kerry Packer against Rupert Murdoch. Fitzy is a prolific producer of books and articles and an extremely funny speaker. He reckons his father once said, 'When it's raining, get all your pots out' and he certainly took his old man's words to heart because when it comes to maximising opportunities, he's in a class of his own. A couple of years ago he had two bestsellers out at the same time: the biography of John Eales and a fascinating story about the New Zealand war hero Nancy Wake, whose exploits had largely been ignored in her home country.

Fitzy's greatest gift is his sense of humour. At times it knows no boundaries but more often it's a reflection of his sharp brain leading to quick witticisms. He's one of the best after-dinner speakers on the circuit, which means he doesn't come cheap. We'd like to use him more on our television programme but simply can't afford him. Some of his rivals criticise him for being mercenary, but I won't buy into that.

Fitzy is the hottest thing on the Australian rugby scene because his wit, his enthusiasm and his seemingly endless energy make him a compelling entertainer. You're never quite sure what's coming next because he doesn't know himself! When I think of FitzSimons, I immediately think of Nick Farr-Jones. They go together like bacon and eggs, Gregan and Larkham, Charlotte Dawson and publicity. Fitzy is over the top in his praise of Nick: 'I'd walk over broken bottles for him but I wouldn't cross the road to save Campo [David Campese] if he'd pulled a hamstring and a truck was about to run over him.'

Nick is a delight. He's shrewd, with very perceptive eyes and a brain that's constantly active. He sent rumblings through my crew when he arrived on set with a bottle of Heineken which he then polished off in double-quick time before ordering another one. Not the done thing, but Nick doesn't fit any mould. I thought he was a bit of a hard case until Inga the Winger told me Nick was a committed Christian. When I queried Nick about this, he responded, 'What do you think they were drinking at the Last Supper — water?'

Farr-Jones inevitably provides a dispassionate appraisal of a team's prospects. He and David Kirk, who is a similar type, were the only commentators to accurately predict the outcome of the 2003 World Cup, including the early exit by the All Blacks.

Most New Zealanders think the London *Sunday Times* rugby correspondent Stephen Jones is a prick. No one stirs up the talkback callers as he does. They hate him, detest his arrogance and abhor everything he stands for. The trouble is that Stephen is more often right than wrong. It was Jones who predicted that New Zealand forward play, the basis of our traditional success, would be weakened by the glitzy, no-contact, flossy Super 12 game. He was right. That isn't what gets the talkback lines humming, though. It's the way Stephen says it, with a unique gloating tone that is designed to enrage.

I've hardly used him lately because he seems to think he's bigger than the game. In the introduction to my last interview I referred to him as 'Stephen Jones, the English journalist'. Immediately, Stephen came on air with his nose out of joint. 'You're lucky I haven't hung up on you,' he said haughtily. 'I'm Welsh, not English. It would be like me referring to you as an Australian. How would you like that?' Correspondents are there to report on issues, not give the audience a rundown on their heritage. Jones was being interviewed because he was a rugby authority. In reviewing the tape we reached the conclusion that Stephen had become self-important. I suggested to Greg Billings that he should ring Stephen to clear the air but Billings succinctly summed it up with, 'Stuff him!'

From one extreme of the personality spectrum to the other, Grant Morrison epitomises the salt-of-the-earth Kiwi. He has been on the fringes of radio now for about 20 years dutifully reporting on surf lifesaving and rallying. Grant's favourite word is 'certainly' and he certainly uses it extensively in his reports. Greg and I sit there giggling as we count the number of times he squeezes it in. His absolute gem was a reply to my question that Cory Hutchings was 'on fire' in the iron man. 'Certainly is, Deaks,' he responded. 'You can be certain of one thing, Cory is certainly the bloke to catch.' The use of the word is a mark of Grant's positiveness: he always looks on the bright side of life. He's had his share of health problems but has overcome them by the enthusiastic way he embraces life. A top bloke, certainly.

Mandy White is the yoga queen of the country. The wrong side of 45, Mandy could easily pass for someone in her early 30s. She has an amazing body carefully toned by hours of exhausting work and through total immersion in her anti-ageing philosophy. When she first arrived in the studio I wondered what we'd struck. As an introduction, I boomed, 'Yoga expert Mandy White joins us for the next hour. We'll all be standing on our heads.' Quick as a flash, Mandy was on her feet, bent right over so that her head touched the ground. She spread her legs wide apart, brought her head and her arms between them and waved to me. I knew then we were in for a different hour.

Her next arrival in the studio was even more spectacular. Without any introduction she came to the window between the control room and my studio and did a quick flash. The weather has never sounded so exotic! Mandy is the total enthusiast, completely dedicated to her work. Full of exuberance and zest, she lives on the edge, courting disaster and success with equal enthusiasm. Invariably she attracts about 20 callers an hour, the absolute maximum, all of whom she can 'fix'. I like her but there are times I do wonder who's the host and who's the guest.

George Duncan proved his expertise to me in a practical and spectacular way. I'd been the slowest runner on Takapuna Beach ever since Judge Barry Morris hung up his 'gymmies'. I got slower and slower as my Achilles got worse and worse. Not that I want to leave you with the wrong impression — I was the slowest player to ever appear at lock for Otago. Enter George. It was Graham Henry and John Graham who introduced us. George had been Graham's sport muscle therapist at Auckland and the Blues. When John spotted me limping, even worse than normal, he asked, 'What's wrong?'

'Bloody Achilles,' I replied. 'They want to operate on it. You name them, I've seen them — physios, masseurs, doctors and now a specialist. They all say it's stuffed.'

'You haven't seen me, mate,' growled George. 'I can fix you in six sessions and if I don't, you can have your money back.'

He did better than that. After two sessions, I was walking normally and after six I was running again. George is the maestro, a man with gifted hands who won't have a bar of any of the gadgets that physios now seem to regard as essential. Naturally, he has become a regular on air where listeners lap up his laconic advice. The first time he was on we simply couldn't cope with the calls, so I asked him to give his phone number.

'It's in the book,' he grunted, 'under G for George.' And so he became no longer George Duncan but simply G for George. His success rate with massaging my listeners, both figuratively and literally, is amazing.

G for George is married to J for Jennifer, a Canadian personal trainer who, fortunately, is the opposite of George. You couldn't have two like George. Jennifer has now also become a regular on the show, sharing her knowledge and experience in a totally different but equally effective way. She's certainly much more pleasant to look at.

Brian Kelly has petrol in his veins: he breathes, eats and sleeps motor sport. He follows the main events right through the country. What isn't so widely known is that BK is the highly successful breakfast host of Radio Classic Hits in Tauranga. BK will go to any lengths to obtain an interview. We've all become used to him commentating from the pillion position on a motorbike as he hares after the rally cars.

Four years ago Brian pushed the limits. Along with 500 other journalists, he was covering the Formula One race in Melbourne. He went to the enormous Ferrari press conference where the media were all cutting each other's throats for the definitive exclusive interview. Ferrari wheeled out its stars, Rubens Barrichello and Michael Schumacher. At the conclusion of the conference it was made clear there were not going to be any personal interviews. That didn't stop BK. He hurdled the rope and as Schumacher was walking back to the pits the world's television focused on this funny Kiwi bloke getting the one exclusive. The highlight was Schumacher telling Brian he was 'a very naughty, cheeky chap'.

Graham Agars is an ideal correspondent, intelligent, articulate and knowledgeable, not afraid to engage controversy and state opinions.

His coverage of tennis and golf is always professional and thought-provoking.

Many of our regulars are unpaid. All of them are fanatical about their work and diligent in the extreme. It is their insight, their enthusiasm and their expertise that has made the radio programme much more than just one man's opinion.

Memorable interviews

Wayne Smith is a good person, honest, straight and direct. After the complexities of John Hart he brought a welcome simplicity of personality and purpose to the role of All Black coach. He amassed an enviable record of success with the Crusaders (taking out back-to-back Super 12s) and Canterbury and after acting as technical adviser to the All Blacks in 1999 replaced Hart as coach. The All Blacks were in turmoil when he took them over. Major changes followed the unsuccessful World Cup campaign, particularly in the organisation of the management of the team.

They used the model successfully developed by New Zealand Cricket, with John Graham as manager and Steve Rixon as coach, his responsibilities restricted to team training, tactics and happenings on the field. Graham, a former All Black captain, was part of the panel responsible for Smith's appointment. Ex-army man Andrew Martin was appointed All Black manager and given much wider powers. Against this background it was understandable that the new coaching combination of Wayne Smith and his assistant Tony Gilbert struggled to achieve consistent results.

In 2001, the morning after the team's failure to win the Bledisloe Cup, for a second time, I interviewed Wayne. My broadcast position was a hotel room in Sydney and Wayne, who had just finished a press conference, was in the lobby of a different hotel. The interview remains the most influential I've ever conducted. The questions were standard until I posed the one New Zealand rugby fans wanted answered: 'Wayne, given the failure to win the Bledisloe Cup, do you think you're the right person to coach the All Blacks at the next World Cup?'

There was silence on the other end of the line — not a brief moment of reflection but a protracted silence. Finally, Smith spluttered, 'I don't know.'

A less honest person would never have answered that way. On another occasion, at a different time or even in a face-to-face interview he may have answered differently. Too late. The moment he said it the consequences were always going to be far-reaching. Our talkback lines back in the studio in Auckland went berserk. An outraged New Zealand public quickly blamed the defeat on Smith. Here was a coach who wasn't sure he wanted to be in charge of the All Blacks. For the average rugby fan this was tantamount to the Pope wanting to pull out of the papacy.

The print media picked up on the interview and speculation became rife. Eventually, Smith reapplied for the coaching job but his indecisiveness had been witnessed by an entire sporting nation and he was sacked, to be replaced by John Mitchell. Some of my colleagues in the media have suggested I should be shot for my role in all of this. Unlike his successor, Wayne Smith was pleasant, polite and usually available for interviews.

Some listeners remain annoyed with me. One said, 'If you hadn't asked Wayne that question he would still have remained coach of the All Blacks.' That may be true, but it's my job to ask that type of question. How the individual deals with it is over to him. The fact Wayne couldn't answer it positively highlighted the fact he wasn't equipped to handle all aspects of what is an onerous role.

He knew immediately he'd blown it. A TV 3 crew was waiting to record an interview with him and was surprised when the usually mild-mannered Smith declared at the end of our conversation, 'That guy's nothing but an arsehole.'

The interviewer asked, 'Oh, who was that?'

'Bloody Deaker.'

Buck Shelford, a good friend of Smith, told me Wayne now couldn't stand me, which is unfortunate. But tough questioning, particularly after a test defeat, goes with the territory for an All Black coach. I simply asked the question; the rest was over to Smith.

Greg Murphy is the best New Zealand sportsman to interview. He bubbles with energy, enthusiasm, zest and humour. The moment he comes on air listeners are lining up to talk with him, with Dean of

Pukekohe always top of the list. Like Murph, Dean is a Holden fan but his brother drives Fords. This led to Dean telling Murph and the nation that his brother was free to a good home while the much-abused sibling could be heard screaming profanities in the background. Murph is a sponsor's dream. He drops Holden and K-Mart into the conversation without missing a beat. He believes he learned the technique from Peter Brock, who for many years dominated the V8 scene on and off the track.

The only All Blacks to rival Murph would be Andrew Mehrtens and Marc Ellis. Unfortunately, Ellis was never prominent enough in his sport to be featured regularly when he was playing. And bone-headed administrators have stifled Mehrts, frightened he might actually say something. They instruct their media prevention officers to ensure he is always unavailable.

Generally, those involved in individual sports are much better to talk to than those playing team sports. Sadly, rugby players have become nearly the worst. For that, we can blame the media liaison officers. Initially, MLOs were appointed to ease the media's job. Unfortunately, the exact opposite has happened. Their respective rugby unions pay these people and the old cliché of 'he who pays the piper calls the tune' certainly applies. They have become universally known as media prevention officers whose prime function seems to be to drive a wedge between the players and the media. They're almost all figures of ridicule, powerless at getting players to cooperate and incapable of making decisions.

Rugby's image has suffered drastically as a result. During the last World Cup campaign a talkback caller from Christchurch, Laurie, explained that he had been a lifetime supporter of the All Blacks but no longer felt part of them. 'I can never forgive John Mitchell for taking them away from me,' he said. 'We're no longer part of them . . .'

If this continues, rugby will soon cease to be the working person's game. Already ticket prices are so exorbitant the average punter can't afford to attend. The average price of tickets for the 2003 World Cup was $1,100 or, more simply put, $15 a minute. Since most games are lucky if they have 30 minutes of actual action, the punters are effectively forking out $40 a minute. If rugby wants to retain its supporters, they have to be able to identify with the players. If they can't afford to attend the major matches and can't see or hear their favourite players being interviewed, it won't be long before they're supporting individuals in a rival code, who are prepared to front up to the media.

It isn't that the All Blacks are short on intelligence. When you do get an opportunity to talk to them, you find they're personable, intelligent individuals, often with interesting observations to make. Trouble is, many have been poisoned by the current policy. Instead of devising ways and regulations to prevent players from talking, the MLOs should be training the players in interview techniques. Being a professional player carries certain obligations, both on and off the field. In the United States failure to fulfil these obligations leads to fines, and in some cases dismissals. In New Zealand, rugby players get away with doing the bare minimum to promote the game, their shoddy behaviour often explained away as being caused by stress. What rubbish! If they feel that way, let them go back to their half-finished phys. ed. diplomas or their labouring jobs that returned a fraction of the healthy salaries they receive to play rugby, a 'job' most labourers would give their eye teeth to secure.

Rugby league players are as bad, but at least they try. It's easier to get access to them but why does every second word have to be 'mate'? The Ropati boys, Hugh McGahan, Frank Endacott and Tony Iro have demonstrated that not all league types are monosyllabic boofheads, incapable of analysis and evaluation. Again, it's surprising how little media training league players are given. Internationally, the game is almost a nonevent and for it to thrive in Australasia it needs constant media coverage. The best ambassadors or public relations officers for a game are its leading players.

In 2003, Mario Andretti visited New Zealand to promote Caltex. Andretti is living proof of the American dream. He arrived in the United States from Italy as a child unable to speak English but he was always going to make it in some area of human endeavour. Fortunately for motor sports fans, his family settled next door to a dirt track and, as they say in the classics, the rest is history.

He arrived at Newstalk ZB's studio at 6.50 p.m. and we recorded a 10-minute television interview for *Deaker on Sport*. Immediately after that he went live on radio on *Sportstalk* for a 15-minute interview, followed by 45 minutes of talkback. It was only later that I discovered he had agreed to only a 15-minute radio interview. Never once did he complain or indicate I was imposing on his time. Throughout, Andretti was the complete professional. Polite, poised, always in control, reasoned, sincere and genuine, he wooed the public. He was totally unable to understand why some New Zealand sports people were reluctant to talk to the media. 'How do they expect their sport to continue to prosper if they don't make an effort?' he asked.

Occasionally in an interview a pearl is dropped. When asked what he attributed his success to, Mario didn't hesitate. 'I surround myself with good people,' he replied. Perhaps our league and rugby players need better people around them to achieve greater success off the field.

When Gavin Hastings, the former Scottish and British Lions fullback, visited New Zealand with his family just before the 2003 World Cup as a guest of the whisky company The Famous Grouse, he came to my home to record a television interview. Usually, this type of chat reveals little, but out of the blue Hastings fired a memorable shot. When asked about the contribution made to Scottish rugby by the 'kilted Kiwis', big Gav was scathing of John Leslie.

'I've got no time for John,' he said, before outlining the way Leslie had used Scottish football. On the other hand, he was complimentary about John's brother Martin as well as Gordon Simpson and Todd Blackadder. Gavin believed that Jim Telfer and Ian McGeechan had done Scottish rugby a disservice by selecting Brendan Laney for the international team a fortnight after he had arrived in the country. What had been foreseen as an innocuous chat produced a rich talking point. New Zealand fans had been moaning for years about the drain of players to European countries, arguing this weakened our rugby. Now we were hearing complaints that the migration was having a detrimental effect on Scotland's rugby.

Gavin has a brilliant personality and an easy manner with the ladies, which possibly explained why my camerawoman at the interview, my wife Sharon, raced away to get her own camera to have her photo taken on Gavin's knee. The following day the photo was developed, framed and displayed on our table. A memorable interview all round.

Louisa Wall is a strikingly beautiful woman who has embraced feminism and Maori rights, two trendy topics that usually turn me off people. A double New Zealand representative in netball and rugby, Louisa is articulate, outspoken and direct — qualities that make her an exceptional interview subject. But I wasn't prepared for the bomb-shell she dropped when I met her in the wings of the set of *Deaker Profiles*. She proudly introduced me to her 'partner', another woman of equally arresting appearance.

During the interview she 'came out'. The reaction was predictable. Six people sent in vitriolic letters saying they would never watch my programme again. One went as far as suggesting I was a closet homosexual promoting the gay movement. The reaction gave me a first-hand experience of what most gays face most days. If you can judge from what I had written to me it's much easier to be straight. In fact, the interview went some way to changing my personal attitude and reaction to gays, but still didn't adequately prepare me for events that followed soon after in France.

Sharon and I decided we would like to holiday in the Loire Valley with our two oldest offspring, my son James and Sharon's son Bart. Coming along for the memorable bike trip organised by former Auckland rugby coach Maurice Trapp and his wife Gail were James' wife Amy and Bart's wife Rachel. We ended up at a chateau that provided a magnificent vista out over the valley and a fabulous swimming pool.

On the final day James and I were sunning ourselves beside the pool when I noticed an unusual flag flying from the mast atop the chateau. 'What the hell is that flag, James?' I asked.

'Dad, this trip has been a real eye-opener. Apart from the sight of your mate Mike Hutchinson, all seventeen stone of him, on a bike, I can't believe we're in France — as kids you told us to hate it after the blowing up of the *Rainbow Warrior*. Now you choose as our final destination a chateau that's fully staffed and owned by gays. That flag's the symbol of the gay liberation movement.'

For once, I was speechless.

If any reinforcement of James' observation was required, it occurred that night at our journey's wind-up dinner. Both Mike's wife and Sharon, along with the two younger women, were dressed up to the nines but the centre of the waiters' attention was Monsieur Mike. 'What a big man, ooh, aah,' one waiter gurgled. Mike didn't know whether to blush, be angry or crow. For once, he too was speechless.

John Eales' nickname is Nobody, as in 'Nobody is perfect'. It's a mark of the respect his team-mates afford him. In the late 1990s Eales was to Australian rugby what Colin Meads had been to New Zealand in the 1960s — the icon, the benchmark, the legend. More than anything, Eales is a gentleman.

In February 2003, as the World Cup approached, we at Sky were conscious that without rights to the event we would struggle to have sufficient footage to compete with TVNZ. So Greg Billings and I flew to Sydney to interview John O'Neill, Eddie Jones, Rod Macqueen and John Eales, all in the same day. It was a tight schedule, but you do that when you're meeting the expenses yourself.

Eales gave me an hour of his time, claiming goalkicking, forward power and enthusiasm would be the key ingredients required for winning a World Cup — aspects that went unheeded by the All Blacks. As always, John was polite and pleasant, even gentle in his approach. At the conclusion of the interview he helped us pack up the gear, tossing the cumbersome tripod over his broad shoulders like a rugby gear bag and accompanied us down the 20 flights of stairs to the road where he ran across the street to secure us a taxi.

No wonder we in the media continue to emphasise the difference in attitude and demeanour between the Aussies and the All Blacks. A lot of it can be put down to education: most of the leading Wallabies are products of the Australian public school system. But a significant portion can be attributed to the fact that, unlike New Zealand, they are forever competing for media space with Australian Rules, league and soccer.

The All Blacks are light years behind and under John Mitchell they regressed further. The tragedy is that most of the journalists in New Zealand are rugby men, often prepared to overlook rudeness and arrogance in their attempts to get the story. If the Wallabies acted like the All Blacks, Aussie press men like Greg Growden, Peter Jenkins and Peter FitzSimons would rip them to pieces. Chris Moller and Darren Shand, the new All Black manager, have a real challenge on their hands: some of us have had enough.

When Moller came into my studio for a radio interview after the World Cup, I was determined to get answers to the hard questions. Why hadn't the NZRU roped in Mitchell when his treatment of the media and sponsors became so appalling that it alienated large sections of the rugby public? Moller finally agreed this had been a mistake.

What happened off air was more powerful and will have long-term effects. Moller was told in no uncertain terms that I would never again interview Mitchell, on radio or television. I outlined in depth the un-successful attempts my producers had made over a period of 12 months to get Mitchell to air. We had been demeaned, embarrassed, frustrated and had wasted hours of valuable time. Never again.

Rod Macqueen is another outstanding Australian rugby personality who recognised the importance of keeping onside with the media. Macqueen was unquestionably the rugby coach of the 1990s and deserves to rank up there with the giants of the past like Fred Allen and Carwyn James.

In a television interview in February 2003, Macqueen, who's also a highly successful businessman, drew interesting parallels between coaching a winning rugby team and running a profitable business. What made it especially poignant was that the points Rod made were precisely those expounded by multi-millionaire entrepreneur Tony O'Reilly, a former Irish and British Lions winger, in an interview with me a few months earlier. Both were clear that businesses and teams need a vision, sound professional practices, accountability, worthy plans to institute the vision and, most important of all, the involvement of quality individuals. It isn't rocket science, just good common sense emphasising the need for man management.

A further illustration of the availability of the Australians occurred during the 1991 Rugby World Cup in the UK. To the New Zealand media the All Blacks had become the Untouchables, a team perceived as arrogant and ignorant. Just before the semifinal between the All Blacks and the Wallabies in Dublin, I attempted to interview Simon Poidevin, the feisty Wallaby who served the Aussies so well in more than 50 tests. Someone called Tim answered the phone call to his room. Simon wasn't in but Tim Horan gave me a 20-minute interview, extracts from which were used on national news for the next two days.

The 2003 All Black World Cup squad's general attitude to the media was illustrated at a media day organised at an Auckland hotel before the team advanced to Australia. Sharon and I took the camera along and obtained interviews with Carl Hoeft, Daniel Carter, Rodney So'oialo and Greg Somerville. As we were leaving, I ran into John Mayhew, who'd been the All Black doctor for more than a decade. I asked if I could interview him about the injuries in the team. He said it would be all right if I cleared it with the MLO, Matt McIlraith. So, with my back to Mayhew, I sought approval from McIlraith to conduct the interview.

I was declined. Sharon, watching from a distance, said that while I was confronting McIlraith, Mayhew was shaking his head from side to side. He didn't want to do the interview. Here was a professional, the longest surviving member of the All Black squad, telling you one thing to your face and then instructing the media prevention officer to the contrary. John had obviously been there too long and been bitten by the media malaise bug.

The most disappointing relationship I've experienced with a top sportsman is that with Jeff Wilson, one of that rare breed of individuals who has represented his country in both rugby and cricket. We started on a high. Spiro Zavos, a Sydneysider who remains intensely loyal to New Zealand, having spent a large portion of his life here, rang me in a state of great excitement back in the early 1990s.

Zavos usually only gets excited about the prospect of a free meal, so I listened when he told me he'd just seen the best rugby prospect to come out of New Zealand since George Nepia. He'd been watching the New Zealand schools against their Australian counterparts in Sydney and a fair-haired kid from Southland named Jeff Wilson had cut the Aussies to ribbons.

I interviewed Jeff upon his return, getting our relationship off on a positive note. His mother even requested a tape of the interview. For some time, we continued on a friendly basis, although I gradually became aware that Jeff was becoming precious. He was particularly annoyed with criticisms I'd been directing at the underachievements of the Otago and Highlanders teams and their worrying emphasis on player power.

Things came to a head when he announced exclusively in a patsy interview with TV3 that he was taking a break from the game. This was big news and my producer tried everything in his power to get Jeff on air, to no avail. Consequently, I went on *Sportstalk* that evening and criticised him for his unwillingness to talk to other elements of the media. I concluded by saying, 'Like other All Blacks, Jeff Wilson will be knocking on our doors when he wants publicity for his next book. Well, there's one door he doesn't need to knock on.'

Sure enough, when Jeff's biography was produced, his publishers were keen for me to interview him. And why wouldn't they be? The same company had sold 960 books through an 0800 number during the hour I'd interviewed John Hart about his book.

A meeting was arranged at my home and Jeff arrived with Raewyn Davies, the publicist who had accompanied me throughout New Zealand when we were promoting my book *The Man in the Glass*. I'd decided to back down but I'd had a gutsful of precious All Blacks and I was prepared to let Jeff sweat. I opened by telling him I wasn't happy about the way he'd handled his announcement.

Jeff reacted, letting it all come out. His grievance was that I'd upset many of his playing mates in Otago by criticising their play. The poor things! His biggest gripe was that I'd unmercifully attacked John Hart. It turned out that he'd had dinner with Harty the previous evening and had been convinced that I'd ruined Hart's life by 'character assassination'. While Raewyn stood by, helpless to do or say anything, Jeff declared that he didn't want me to have anything to do with his book. As 3000 certain additional sales disappeared through a bout of petulance Raewyn's face was a sight to behold.

Jeff remains a player for whom I have much admiration, but his comments highlighted yet again the preciousness of our top rugby players. So many of them are pathetically ill-equipped to compromise or make sensible commercial decisions.

From the ridiculous to the sublime. Jeff Walker is a name few New Zealand sports fans will be familiar with, yet he represented this country in swimming, water polo and surf lifesaving. A friend of his from Christchurch told me he was suffering from cancer. Would I present a profile, to give his kids something to treasure? Jeff arrived in Auckland two weeks later on a high: he'd just been given an all clear. We were able to focus on his battle with cancer and his message was emotionally moving, revealing an individual of great character and fortitude. It was sad to learn of his death a year later, but I hope his kids will be able to play the video and understand what a courageous man their father was.

When my producer Greg Billings and I went to Australia to compile a series of *Deaker Profiles*, we encountered some unexpected hazards. During a fascinating discussion with the Australian cricketer Michael Slater in the middle of the Sydney Cricket Ground, the sprinklers went off. We had no sooner launched into an interview with league boss John Ribot than a helicopter began hovering overhead, the pilot apparently curious to know who the personality was in front of the camera lens.

It has been my pleasure over the years to interview such greats as

Carl Lewis, Raelene Boyle, Imran Khan, Ian Botham, Colin Meads, Brian (now Sir Brian) Lochore, Bryan Williams, Inga 'The Winger' Tuigamala, Kevin Skinner and, of course, Bert Sutcliffe.

Bert was my hero — humble, witty, a man of old-fashioned values, polite, sincere and honest. On and off the field, he was an inspiration. A reluctant interview subject, Bert never wanted to talk about himself, yet on just one occasion I wound him up enough to extract the full story about his famous last-wicket partnership in South Africa with Bob Blair, the day after Blair's fiancée had been killed in the Tangiwai disaster. The best questions are simple ones. 'Bert,' I asked, 'what happened that day?'

Bert's reply took eleven and a half minutes during which he graphically described being struck on the head by a bouncer from fast bowler Neil Adcock and how he returned to the ground swathed in bandages. As the blood seeped through and dripped on to the pitch, Bert launched into a ferocious assault upon the South African bowlers.

He didn't expect he would still be batting because he presumed Blair, given the tragic circumstances, would not be coming to the crease. But Blair did come out. Bert described the eerie silence that enveloped the ground when Blair first emerged. It was followed by spontaneous applause, with even the South African players joining in.

If Sutcliffe and Blair had capitulated for a handful of runs, it would have been entirely understandable. Instead, they combined in a valiant last-ditch stand in which the fearless Sutcliffe clobbered several sixes. When the innings finally ended, they received a standing ovation. It remains one of the most memorable and heart-wrenching occasions in New Zealand sport.

The interview was repeated on Sky Sports at least six times after his death. It remains my favourite.

Bert differed so much from many modern sportspeople. He viewed those of us in the media as blokes doing a job and he left us to write, or say, what we wanted. It was a reflection of his outlook on life that he befriended us and made us feel part of the team. His attitude helped to build strong relationships, trust and an understanding of our respective roles. I knew where I stood with Bert. The relationship had been built over 40 years, from schoolboy fan to journalist on my part and from hero to hero on his.

It's appropriate to end this chapter by revealing how such a relationship manifests itself. When Bert died, I presented a eulogy on air and his son Gary asked me to repeat it at the funeral. It shows that sportspeople and the media can grow together and that we both have our place and our uses.

EULOGY TO BERT SUTCLIFFE

Gary, when you asked me to speak at Bert's funeral, I experienced the full range of emotions that a third former would when called in to open the batting for the first eleven — apprehension, anticipation, fear, yet at the same time, pride tempered with humility. Thank you for the honour.

Most of all I feel responsibility to adequately express on behalf of so many people how we feel about Bert.

In the past few days I have read the warm tributes by Don Cameron in the *New Zealand Herald* and John Coffey in the Christchurch *Press* and I've listened to hundreds of callers to radio expressing their views as fans, cricket lovers or just plain old Joe Public.

I've heard the respect in the voices of famous New Zealand cricketers, all of whom obviously regarded Bert as a prince of players, and I heard members of his family, former schoolmates and close friends all share their love for this wonderful man, Bert Sutcliffe, sportsman and gentleman.

As with so many others, Bert was my hero and it's in that capacity I want to address him. Heroes never die; their deeds live on long after they've gone. Heroes are classical, stylish, assured, yet modest, sincere and honest. Bert Sutcliffe was a hero. A hero does heroic things that we mere mortals dream about:

- 385 runs for Otago against Canterbury in 1952;
- smashing Neil Adcock and the other South African bowlers all over Ellis Park on Boxing Day 1953 after he himself had been smashed to the deck by a vicious Adcock bouncer;
- scoring countless centuries, double centuries and even a number of triples.

A hero never blows his cool, is always in control. Bert was. That lovely grin, that knowing look, that wise nod.

A hero always has time for his fans. Bert did, hours of it. The same questions, all the requests for autographs and speaking, all treated with dignity, with warmth, with a human touch.

Heroes can never do any wrong. Bert didn't. Not if you listen to his hundreds of mates, to all the people who hardly knew him but whose lives he touched. Add me to the list of people who've never heard a bad word said about Bert Sutcliffe.

Heroes become part of one's own life experiences. I'll always think of Bert whenever I heard that lovely thud of leather on willow, the smell of linseed oil or watch a left-hander rock back gracefully and hook the ball to the boundary.

I'll particularly think of him at two grounds. One is the front field at Takapuna Grammar School where he learned his craft. Don Coleman, who was in the all-conquering first eleven there with Bert, used to relate delightfully about Bert's batting. Heroes never need to tell you of their own exploits. Don vowed and declared that Bert once hit an on-drive from Takapuna Grammar's front ground to the Belmont shops.

Now, I paced that out. It's about half a mile, uphill! Don reckoned it went along the ground all the way, too. Give it a few more years and the ball will be arriving at the Devonport shops!

The other ground was Carisbrook. Bert, you were King of Carisbrook and we were your loyal servants. Those wonderful days of the early fifties, the summers of our youth, lazy, hazy days.

You glowed. We pinned our hopes on you and you defied the foes from England, Australia, Canterbury, Wellington and Auckland.

Occasionally you failed but umpires made mistakes then too. You were so much part of our lives, our hopes and our aspirations. We idolised you. You were a sportsman in every sense of the word.

In later life we've continued to watch you. A gentle man and a gentleman, quiet, polite with a wonderful sense of humour, immaculate and polished in appearance, sincere, honest and straight in all your dealings with others. You reminded us of what our mothers used to say to us when we were kids: 'Treat others the way you would like to be treated yourself.'

You were a team man first, a gifted individual second. Your name will always be associated with integrity.

Bert Sutcliffe, sportsman and gentleman. Our game, our sport, our community, our nation has been a better place because of you. You have enriched our lives.

Heroes never die. Their deeds live on long after they've gone.

Best in the business

Leighton Smith and Paul Holmes are patently the best radio broad-casters in New Zealand. Their styles differ but they're equally effective.

Leighton is logical, analytical, right-wing and hard-hitting. Paul is emotive, subjective, populist and unpredictable. Of the two, Leighton has had a greater impact on me. He's prepared to take stances, no matter how unpopular these may be.

Paul is an expert at gauging public opinion — in fact, he's often ahead of it — and at running with it. It would be an exaggeration to say he runs with the hares and hunts with the hounds. Leighton is his own man, forthright and strong. He's prepared to attack the sacred cows of New Zealand society. His recent attack on Maori nepotism, on Maori television rorts and on the ridiculous claim for the Queen's chain were stances of the kind other broadcasters avoid.

What Paul possesses, which Leighton lacks, is a well-developed sense of humour and a wonderful sense of both social and political timing. He's an entertainer first, a broadcaster second, and there are times when he has you rocking with mirth, not something Leighton is capable of. (Broadcasters need, above all, to be entertainers. If they can't capture their audience's attention, they'll go elsewhere. And in Auckland, there are plenty of choices, with around 25 radio stations broadcasting daily.)

Paul's energy and his diligence are admirable. He ad-libs beautifully. How he manages to function so professionally at opposite ends of the day, on breakfast radio in the morning and prime television in the evening, week in, week out, almost defies belief, but is testimony to his strength and his work ethic. At times, his heavy workload affects him, both on and off the air. It was probably this that led to his biggest on-air gaffe, labelling United Nations secretary-general Kofi Annan a 'cheeky darkie'.

In case you were visiting Mars at the time, these excerpts from his broadcast will enlighten you on what he said:

'That Kofi Annan, I've got to say to you, has been a very cheeky darkie overnight. He's been a very cheeky darkie. It's all very well giving a darkie that secretary-general job but we'll only take so much. I'm sorry, we will only take so much. We're not going to be told how to live our lives by a Ghanaian.'

The public furore was predictable and from it two salient points emerged. One was that Paul had plainly got carried away with his own rhetoric. He wound himself up and simply lost it. Now Paul Holmes is many things, but racist he isn't. In fact, one of my criticisms of him in the past has been that in dealing with Maori issues he has too readily trodden the politically correct line.

The second was of much greater interest to me. The broadcasters, hosts and producers at Newstalk ZB generally supported Paul while the news staff (the reporters and readers) were generally critical of him. A number of my fellow hosts took pains to explain that 'they' didn't understand 'us'.

From a personal viewpoint, the cheeky darkie saga was a timely reminder of how close to the edge we are when constantly behind the microphone. Paul crossed the line and his reputation and status will be affected for the rest of his career. Another such indiscretion would have him packing his bags and retreating to his hideaway in Hawke's Bay.

It will be interesting to watch Paul's approach to difficult issues. Will he be able to walk the tightrope again? Warwick Roger, one of New Zealand's outstanding print journalists, never recovered his sharp edge after a prolonged litigation battle with fellow journalist Toni McRae.

Paul is tough, though, which is just one of the characteristics that have made him such a successful broadcaster. Like a lot of entertainers, he's prepared to wear his heart on his sleeve. When he's at his best, he's outstanding, particularly when he projects his humanitarian side to people who are suffering. Mostly, he has used his power and his position to assist individuals, rather than shoot them down. At the same time, Paul is capable of hard, uncompromising interviews that can be extremely entertaining. He seems to save his best for Winston Peters, or is that Winnie knows how to press his buttons?

Leighton Smith is a good bloke, forthright in the extreme, opinionated beyond belief, widely read and, at times, exquisitely articulate. Over the years, Leighton has had a much bigger impact on me than he would ever have thought — not that I seek him out for advice. At times, though, I listen carefully to Leighton and if I've developed some calmness now in my debates with callers, it's largely through adopting the techniques that Leighton has perfected. He's fortunate to be produced by Carolyn Leaney, who is the perfect foil for him when he's too high or too low. She's hard-working, totally committed to Leighton, well prepared, diligent and experienced.

There are only two other broadcasters within a bull's roar of Paul and Leighton. They are Larry Williams and Martin Devlin.

Williams is the hardest working broadcaster I've come across. Nothing is left to chance. Larry puts in long hours: he's always at work around 11 a.m. for his 4 p.m. to 7 p.m. drive show. From the moment he walks in, he's hard at it, researching the Net, the papers and anything else he can lay his hands on. Like a dog with a bone, he gnaws away till he gets the result he believes is warranted. (Diligence is essential in this business. Pam Corkery and her producer sister Adele certainly made an amazing amount of noise but their heads were always down as they sought to cover all bases.) Larry sees things in black and white. A couple of years ago he did some university papers and I hope he'll return to study. It would broaden his view and allow him to better appreciate the other side of the argument. As a broadcaster, he does claim one dubious honour: he's the most proficient thrower of golf clubs ever to grace the airwaves.

Competitiveness, ambition, zeal and the desire to be the best in the business are all qualities a top broadcaster must possess. If you're away from your seat for too long, a rival might settle in. I now strive harder than ever before to be the best sports broadcaster in New Zealand, and when people ask me what keeps me going, I answer, 'Martin Devlin'. The voice of Radio Sport arrived on the scene at a time when I was clearly number one. At that time his sports knowledge could have been amply displayed on a kicking tee, and there would still have been room for the ball, but Martin is a worker and he has expanded his sporting knowledge by 200 per cent. He's very much in the Holmes mould — unconventional, hard-working, egotistical, quirky and un-predictable. I enjoy listening to him and his new producer, Matt Gunn, has added to the programme. Devlin has the ability to eventually re-place Holmes.

Danny Watson and Kerre Woodham complete the Newstalk ZB team. Danny makes up in enthusiasm what he may lack in expertise while Kerre is keen, energetic and spontaneous. Along with young broad-casters yet to emerge, they will determine the future of Newstalk ZB. Although there are plenty of graduates from the numerous journalism and broadcasting schools, few are showing the qualities needed to reach the top.

Martin Devlin has been a consistent winner of the Best Sports Broad-caster at the radio awards and, although the judging system is flawed, it does reflect the impact he's been making.

What the public doesn't appreciate is that these awards are judged on the 20-minute tape the entrant submits. This is meant to encapsu-late the entrant's work over an entire year but of course, it doesn't. Naturally, everyone sends in what they deem their best 20 minutes of work. Largely, these awards are determined by the technical skill of the person putting the tape together. This isn't sour grapes coming from Deaks. I've won my share of awards but the victories didn't give me the satisfaction they would have if the award had been based on what went to air over an entire year, or a week . . . or even a day. But 20 minutes? Who's kidding who?

For me, the strength of Radio Sport is its live broadcasts, where Allen McLaughlan is the standout commentator. I'm not top of Mac's popularity poll because of the stand I took over the Warriors when they were labouring away in the NRL. Mac has fought for years for an underprivileged game and won't have a bad word said against them, but this chip on his shoulder doesn't stop him calling his games more accurately than anyone else.

Over the years I've sat alongside the best in the world and listened to them commentate while watching the action unfold before my eyes. Even the doyen of rugby commentators, the great Bill McLaren, couldn't match Mac for accuracy and timing. And I don't just mean accuracy in describing the play but in pronouncing the most difficult of Polynesian names. His anticipation of when a try-scoring movement is about to unfold, his enthralling description of events and his resonant voice make him quite simply the best rugby, league or soccer caller that I've heard.

Peter Montgomery is another at the top of his field. Clearly the voice of international yachting, Peter can make the dullest yacht race, and most of them are dead boring, sound like the Thriller in Manila with Ali and Smokin' Joe going head to head. At the conclusion of an America's Cup or a Whitbread series, Pete is worn out, utterly exhausted. Unlike Mac, PJ possesses a great sense of humour. His description of the archaic broadcasting gear we operate with at Newstalk ZB would do Billy Connolly proud.

If Peter is the best commentator yachting has seen, his wife Claudia deserves the ultimate award for tolerating the stressful situations he creates during the big campaigns. The Montgomerys are a tight unit. I'm an admirer of Pete's son Johnny, who was born prematurely. Peter takes him everywhere and sister Katie tolerates Johnny's hype. Born into any other family, I doubt Johnny Montgomery would be the fine young man he has developed into. Peter isn't only an excellent commentator, he's a top dad, a bloke with excellent values. And he possesses a grand command of the English language as well. In an industry where gossip and innuendo flourish, Peter stands tall, above it all. We've been through a lot together, and I've pushed the boundaries several times, but I always look forward to my next encounter with PJ.

Graeme Moody, Radio Network's eager and energetic rugby commentator, seems able to survive on desperately little sleep and catered sandwiches for an entire World Cup. 'Moods' works his butt off in trying to keep every tinpot station in the network happy. When it comes to diligence and resilience, he's near the top of the stack.

Mike Hosking could be a topline broadcaster. His diction, intellect, timing and general knowledge put him in an elite bracket. But he lacks an essential ingredient that Paul Holmes possesses in liberal amounts: soul. Mike has been the victim of the worst of gutter press. No one deserves the treatment he received from that 18-year-old who stalked him or the *Sunday News* who wouldn't let up on his private life. Mike needs a holiday, a break of at least a year from a job at which he could be brilliant.

Melodie Robinson has graduated from being a talented Black Fern, part of the team that twice won the women's Rugby World Cup, to fronting on television. Attractive, intelligent, bright and enthusiastic, she could make it in any market in the world. A former Miss Canterbury, she is photogenic, an adjective no one ever applied to me. Possessed of a university degree, she is feisty, aggressive and self-assured — a real talent.

Mel represented the biggest risk I ever took on television. After she'd joined us on *Deaker on Sport* as a guest to discuss the Black Ferns, she asked if I thought she had a future in TV. We decided to try her in the Holden Chat Room. Unfortunately, most of the oddballs who e-mailed her only wanted to take her to bed.

Callers jammed the lines with comments like, 'Get that bitch off the air' and 'Has Deaks gone mad?' We protected her from those reactionary calls and the rest is history. She now regularly hosts the build-up to major matches on the Sky channel and her confidence grows daily. I confidently predict that she'll be a top sports broadcaster of the future. That gives me great pleasure, because John McCready, the former boss of TVNZ, advised me to get her off air. John is rarely wrong, but on this occasion he clearly was.

Willie Lose is another success story. There are few nicer people on this planet than Willie, who as a loose forward of not inconsiderable talent represented Tonga at the 1999 World Cup. He desperately wants to achieve success in his new vocation, and he might. It won't be for want of trying. He works his butt off, overpreparing, overanalysing and being overanxious, all admirable qualities in a young broadcaster. And he listens, which is another quality not possessed by all young trainees. But he's too nice to everyone. I'll know Willie has made it the day he tells a caller he's talking drivel and to get off the line.

The other rugby player to make an impact as a sports presenter in 2003 was former All Black Ian Jones. 'Kamo' knows his stuff, is passionate about the game and enthusiastic about his role. In fact, he's a breath of fresh air, especially when you compare his expert comments with those of Murray Mexted, who is forever harping on about refereeing injustices. Andrew Fyfe, the executive producer of Sky, urgently needs to pull Mexted into line, or dismiss him, which would be a shame given Murray's early promise and obvious love of rugby. But he needs help. To digress, when I was introduced to Murray Mexted the first question he asked me was, 'What level of rugby did you play to?' In Murray's insular view of life, if you haven't been an All Black you know little about the game. I wish he would apply that personally. He has never refereed at any level yet that doesn't stop him confusing Sky's viewers about referees' decisions, game after game.

Greg Billings, my long-serving producer of *Scoreboard*, and I probably argue every day and sometimes our disagreements are major. But that's the strength of our relationship. Greg is a complex mixture of cynicism, humanity, intelligence and street sharpness. He can make instantaneous decisions, which is crucial in his role, and they're almost always correct.

Tim Bickerstaff, the trailblazer of sporting talkback shows in New Zealand but these days marketing products that guarantee to put the x back into sex, once said, 'Deaker is only successful because of Billings.' What is clear is that the Billings–Deaker partnership had stood the test of time. He now produces *Deaker on Sport* on Sky TV as well. He's loyal, honest and direct, and possesses a great sense of humour. Quite simply, Greg Billings is the best sports producer in New Zealand, by a very wide margin.

That doesn't necessarily mean that the same formula will be successful on television. For eight years Greg produced and I presented *Deaker Profiles*, which was really radio with pictures. *Deaker on Sport* fell into the same category until my wife, Sharon, as executive producer, began meddling. Initially, she infuriated me with her concepts for change, but she doesn't give up easily. She was acutely aware of the programme's weaknesses and kept promoting the idea of involving a line producer, someone skilled who would convert our performance into a genuine television show.

The recommended individual was Mark Casey with whom she had worked at Communicado. I have to confess to a certain uneasiness when I first encountered him because he has the best head of hair I've ever seen on a male. But Sharon was determined, and Mark joined us at the beginning of 2003.

In the wake of the collapse of Communicado, Mark had formed his own one-man television company, True Colours. He concedes he knows precious little about sport but he possesses a wonderful feel for television. His creative flair, inherent logic and basic common sense immediately distinguished him as a television producer of exceptional quality, the best it's been my privilege to work with.

Mark Casey is a good man with high values. He was the only person in the industry Sharon took into her confidence when I was in the depths of depression. Mark would never break a confidence. She said to him, 'Murray needs you in his ear right through the programme. Don't worry what anyone in the production team thinks or says.' Mark didn't worry. Without him, I doubt I would have made it through. I hope his immense talent will be recognised because I feel he has the potential to succeed in films or major documentaries.

Few former sportsplayers make it in broadcasting, although some are adept as comments people: former All Blacks Grant Fox and John Drake slot into this category. But the outstanding exception is Ian Smith, whose performance on television is attaining the same soaring heights that marked his glove work when he was the New Zealand test wicketkeeper. In just a few short years he's progressed to being one of the most accomplished and celebrated cricket commentators not just in New Zealand but on the world circuit. Such is his versatility he's also become an outstanding sideline eye at rugby matches and is a most competent interviewer and presenter. The reason so few players have succeeded as commentators in New Zealand could be because the country is so small they find it inhibiting when criticising former team-mates. This plainly isn't a problem across the ditch in Australia where former greats like Richie Benaud, Bill Lawry, Ian Chappell and the Channel 9 crew are always prepared to slag off today's cricketers when they falter — which, admittedly, isn't often.

Danny Morrison has brought his cricket expertise and enthusiasm to radio. He has a pleasant voice and is confident behind the microphone but finds it impossible ever to attack a caller and consequently his future may lie mainly in commentary work. He remains a close friend, always offering a joke as he breezes through life.

With Television New Zealand struggling for credibility in sport and given the scarcity of experienced television sports reporters in this country, it's surprising that it was prepared to let go of Richard Becht, the sports editor for the six o'clock news bulletin for almost two decades. Richard certainly knows his sport, having written more than a dozen books and been sports editor of the now defunct *Auckland Sun* newspaper. Together, he and John McCready, the former head of TVNZ's programmes, were largely responsible for popularising league. Both have a genuine love of the 13-man code and Richard used to delight in leading the sports news with league stories.

Marc Ellis has enjoyed phenomenal success and now has a cult following. Unquestionably, he's a genuine talent who would succeed anywhere. At his best he's extremely funny and highly entertaining, though he does need to learn to laugh at himself. The real test for Ellis will be if and when he decides to switch his attention to serious presenting and interviewing. At the moment, he's in danger of being typecast as a clown and he's more than that. I rank him as the personality with the greatest potential on New Zealand television. Can that extraordinary talent be channelled into a disciplined structure?

It's early days yet but I'm thrilled with the progress my younger son John is making in the industry. He possesses an encyclopaedic knowledge of sport, has unbridled enthusiasm and sufficient arrogance to make it as a sports producer. His research on my behalf has lifted both my radio and television programmes to a new level.

Sir Howard Morrison delights in telling you he survived at the top because of three qualities — attitude, attitude and attitude. Those who succeed in the radio industry have the right attitude and they work hard.

Graham Henry

Chris Doig delights in describing Graham Henry as the greatest over-achiever he's known, which really cheeses Henry off. It shouldn't, because there's no greater compliment you can pay someone. (As an aside, a surgeon I'd gone through Otago University with claimed I was the greatest underachiever he had ever met. Now that really was something to be cheesed off about, given that he made the statement shortly after I'd been named Sports Broadcaster of the Year. Obviously, the medical profession doesn't rate radio presenters.)

If Henry is ever reincarnated, and perish the thought, it will be as a terrier — which would make him a hell of a lot faster than he's been this time round. He may lack a terrier's swiftness but he's always possessed one of its other special traits, tenacity. He never lets up for a moment, always probing for another angle to attack until he's mastered the challenge.

Doig knows Henry pretty well. They attended Christchurch Boys' High at the same time and later taught together under John (DJ) Graham at Auckland Grammar. Graham has had a huge influence on both of them, particularly Henry. In fact, after he struggled through his University Entrance examination, he decided to follow in DJ's footsteps by seeking a BA in history. DJ would have none of that and commanded him to pursue a phys. ed. degree at Otago University.

It was while he was studying in Dunedin that I encountered Graham Henry. We became team-mates in the university senior cricket side. The previous year he had represented Canterbury as a wicketkeeper and somehow went on to open the batting for Otago. It wasn't an inspired selection; in fact, remarkably, he effected more catches and stumpings than he scored runs. But it was affirmation of Doig's theory.

Henry was the slowest first-five Otago senior club rugby had ever seen, and that's saying something, given the clumsy, leaden-footed blokes who operated in the position. It didn't stop him sidestepping me once to score in the Rose Stand corner, a memory that haunts me still.

At that time I was very much King of the Forum, an informal meeting in the common room where students got up and abused anyone from the President of the United States to the university chaplain. Henry must have observed me in action a couple of times because he sidled up to me in the café and asked about 'this public-speaking thing'. It was a distinguishing characteristic of the man: he's never hesitated to ask advice. He's remained a better listener than a talker and knows almost instinctively where to turn for counsel.

It's his dogged determination that identifies him as a man of steel. Once he's set his mind to a project, nothing stops him. He is shrewd, streetwise and would call on the devil if he thought that would assist the cause. In everything he takes on, he sets his sights almost impossibly high.

It was the same in teaching, the career he pursued after an unsuccessful business venture. John Graham gave him his big break by appointing him to teach phys. ed. at Auckland Grammar. Henry recognised that the principal's job was beyond reach unless he improved his qualifications, so he slogged his way through a correspondence degree at Massey University and after a stint as deputy principal became headmaster of Kelston Boys' High School.

All Black and Samoan international Inga Tuigamala and Tongan international turned radio personality Willie Lose were both pupils at Kelston during that time and reckon Graham did a first-class job. In typical Henry fashion he assessed the strengths of the school and built on them. Kelston became the powerhouse of boys' sports in Auckland, the rugby and soccer teams winning an almost embarrassing number of titles.

Willie goes further, saying Graham learned how to deal with Polynesians and extract the best from them. He simply did what he always does, worked his butt off to be the very best headmaster he could be. On a number of occasions he demonstrated compassion for the underdog, those struggling in difficult situations and those in a mess. Henry is a closed mouth who knows when and how to retain a confidence, a quality that endeared him especially to young Polynesians. Many of them were fragile in their early stages of puberty and didn't need their 'secrets' being bandied about.

During his headmastership he revealed the other great quality that would distinguish his career: he always surrounds himself with quality individuals.

Steve Cole was a kid we had taught at Auckland Grammar and Henry identified in him the same relentless desire to succeed and please. Steve was appointed deputy principal and slogged his way through years of 12-hour days. Another Steve, Steve Watt the Otahuhu Adding Machine, who was Auckland rugby's most prolific points scorer until a certain Grant Fox came along, succeeded Cole as deputy head and later took over as headmaster.

Graham Henry had the ability not only to choose good people but to extract the best from them. With him terrorising them, the cruisers rapidly became hard workers. Ambition is a much-maligned quality: if you don't want to be the best you never will be. Henry has always wanted to be the best; he's never prepared to accept second best. If it hadn't been education and rugby in which he chose to prosper, he would have made it in business, or whatever else challenged him. He's one of the most ambitious people I've met, never satisfied with being in the wings, always pushing ahead.

Ambition can be a killer for lazy people or those who think they should succeed as of right. But that's not Graham Henry. Diligence is his middle name. He's happiest when he's been set an almost impossible task and he's hacking into it. He spends countless hours analysing videos not only of his own team but also of the opposition. Once that homework is completed he formulates a game plan and trains his team accordingly.

The first signs of Henry's exceptional ability came with his coaching of the Auckland Grammar First XV. If you're thinking that that was kids' stuff, you couldn't be more wrong. Grammar operated a flat backline before anyone outside Australia had thought about it. He had the players to make it operate. The first-five was Nicky Allen, that wonderfully gifted individual who went on to represent the All Blacks in 1980 before his life was tragically cut short. He gave way to the incomparable Grant Fox. At fullback and wing were Gary Henley-Smith and Peter Beguley, who had finished first and second in the senior men's 100-metre sprint at the New Zealand athletic championships in 1975.

With players like John Drake, John McDermott, John Mills and, eventually, the Whetton twins, Gary and Alan, upfront Grammar smashed teams over before the backs ran rampant. Henry was a lateral thinker even in those days. He had his five-eighths and centre virtually standing still and sending the ball to the speedsters outside. It resulted in truckloads of runaway tries.

I'd left Auckland Grammar under a cloud — John Graham sacked me, having previously warned me about the amount I was drinking — but I was drawn back every Saturday afternoon, enthralled by the innovation and skill displayed by Henry's First XV.

With his next appointment, Graham demonstrated that he could adapt his team plan to suit his player assets. The University Club team he prepared had Fox at first-five and possessed a powerful set of forwards that included a young Sean Fitzpatrick. The varsity forwards demolished their opposition while Foxy kept them rolling ahead with his cultured boot. Within three seasons University was celebrating Gallaher Shield success.

Graham's raw ambition came through when in 1990 he daringly challenged Maurice Trapp and Bryan Williams for the Auckland coaching job. This would have been understandable had they been faltering but at the time Henry offered his services Auckland was the NPC champion, held the Ranfurly Shield and the previous season had won 19 matches out of 19, including a famous victory over the Wallabies. Henry failed to displace them but he'd registered his intent and 12 months later, albeit by a narrow margin, he was appointed coach of Auckland. The rest, as they say, is history.

Graham regrets the way he went about displacing Trapp and Williams. It became messy and grubby, and he threw most of the mess and grub. Both Maurice and Beegee were hurt by comments made at the time and by Graham's lobbying. It was a mistake Henry learned from and when John Mitchell embarked on a smear campaign against him in 2003, as they contested the All Black coaching position, he experienced what Messrs Trapp and Williams had gone through a decade earlier.

Graham's successes and achievements with Auckland and the Blues are well documented in Bob Howitt's book *Graham Henry, The X Factor*. I'll concentrate on just one game that vividly illustrates his exceptional qualities as a coach.

In 1995 Auckland journeyed south to Lancaster Park with a 50–50 chance of lifting the Ranfurly Shield. The two sides boasted an equal number of All Blacks but the home advantage was generally expected to get the Cantabs home.

The difference was in the teams' preparations. Canterbury, coached by Vance Stewart, plainly didn't see any need to deviate from the tactics that had made them virtually invincible when operating in front of their faithful home fans. This suited Graham perfectly. After studying several tapes of Canterbury games, analysing their patterns and scrutinising individual traits, he devised a game plan that would completely shut down the red and blacks. It was practised over and over, and the players bought into it so completely that several have since told me they knew they were going to win. One tactic — which wouldn't work now because the laws have changed — involved the Aucklanders repeatedly, if monotonously, kicking the ball dead so that Canterbury would provide them with counter-attacking opportunities from each 22 restart.

Henry had worked out that Canterbury functioned efficiently only when Andrew Mehrtens had time and space to operate. The Aucks ensured he had neither. Furthermore, they pressured halfback Justin Marshall mercilessly, successfully closing down the red and black juggernaut. It's doubtful either of them has ever played more indifferently or been less effective for their home province. Canterbury was so outmanoeuvred, and out-thought, that it lost by an incredible 35–nil, a record winning margin for a challenging team in the Ranfurly Shield. People involved in that Auckland challenge rate it the best example of rugby coaching they've ever witnessed. The home team was lucky the winning margin wasn't much bigger.

Like all good coaches, Graham Henry is loyal to his players. At one after-match function following Auckland's victory over North Harbour in a feisty NPC final at Takapuna, infamously dubbed the Battle of Onewa, Robin Brooke piddled in an ashtray. There were a number of young women close by at the time, including my daughter. On air the next day I rubbished the match and publicised the Brooke piddle. That night a furious Graham Henry rang me. 'I thought you of all people would have had some empathy, especially after all the high jinks you got up to at varsity,' Graham exploded.

'Listen, bud, I got locked up for one of my escapades and Brooke is bloody lucky he wasn't too,' I yelled back down the phone.

We agreed to differ on that particular incident but it showed Graham was prepared to stand by his players.

The other testy moment in our relationship happened four years later when I received a strong tip. Occasionally you chance on to a scoop and I went to air on Newstalk ZB with the news that Graham Henry had signed with Wales. Immediately, Jackie Maitland, the NZRU press officer, was on the phone saying I didn't know what I was talking about. I persisted and the NZRU threatened to sue or blacklist me, which was a joke anyway, given the union's lack of cooperation. The Henry-for-Wales story ran every 15 minutes.

At the time, Graham was attending an NZRU seminar in Wellington. Finally, Jackie Maitland got him to a phone and he said to me, in a hushed voice, 'What the hell are you trying to do, Deaks, stuff up the best deal of my life?'

I knew we'd hit the jackpot and couldn't wait until Maitland came back on the phone. When she did she was far more conciliatory, something NZRU employees aren't renowned for. We were right and they were wrong: Henry was going. Graham and I reached a deal that if I stopped speculating he would give me the exclusive interview once contract negotiations were completed.

Much as I would have liked that, the issue was so big that if I'd held Graham to our telephone agreement the press would have chewed him up for giving an exclusive to an old mate. Instead, we met at Seamart Restaurant, my city office, and planned the press conference at which all would be revealed.

'What do they want, Deaks?' Graham asked.

'They want the truth. Just stand up and tell them, "I'm off to Wales and I'm going tonight." And one other thing, take Raewyn with you. Most of them have wives and they know these decisions are family ones.'

He did just that. The phrase, 'I'm off to Wales and I'm going tonight' will forever be associated with his name. His candour and directness meant the media and public backed him when the Henry Law, forbidding him to coach again in New Zealand, was introduced. It was rightly seen to be spiteful and vindictive.

Chris Doig and John Graham enjoy telling the story of Graham Henry arriving at Glamorgan's home ground in Cardiff to see the Black Caps play at the Cricket World Cup. The crowd burst into thunderous applause, completely distracting the cricketers. All that was happening was that Graham Henry had been identified. The arrival of the Prince of Wales wouldn't have caused a greater commotion.

For a time he really was King Henry, the Redeemer. The Welsh adored him, and why not? Their team won 11 tests on the trot, including a famous first victory over the Springboks, an even more famous victory over England at Wembley (to deny Clive Woodward's men a grand slam), a spectacular victory over France in Paris for the first time in quarter of a century and an unprecedented series triumph against the Pumas in Argentina.

Sport is full of highs and lows and after soaring to the heights with Wales, Graham hit his low with the British Lions. After winning the first test the team came unstuck following a Joe Roff intercept try in the second test and was nosed out by the Wallabies in the decider in Sydney, when Matt Burke achieved a 100 per cent goal-kicking record while Jonny Wilkinson was astray several times.

Two members of the touring party, English players Matt Dawson and Austin Healey, were critical of Graham's coaching methods and selection policies — it should be recorded that they were also critical of assistant coaches Andy Robinson and Phil Larder and manager Donal Lenihan — and a video released some months later showed him in a bad light. I've seen this video and couldn't believe the number of obscenities Graham uttered. He's not normally a foul-mouthed person but the video portrayed him as a grumpy, rather vindictive, crass dictator.

The Lions management understood they had the right of veto on any parts of the video they found unacceptable but the many segments they requested be removed duly appeared in the finished product. You can be sure Graham Henry won't be giving approval to any behind-the-scenes videos of All Black campaigns after that experience.

Graham brings to the All Blacks a wealth of experience, an excellent record and an ability to get good people to work for a common goal. His decision to run with Steve Hansen and Wayne Smith is a brave one on both fronts. Hansen is as ambitious as Henry but still has some way to go. However, it won't be long before he's angling for the top job. Smith cracked under pressure the last time but that won't happen again. He's older, more mature, less intense. Frankly, it's difficult to think of a better appointment.

Graham's biggest attribute is his wife Raewyn. She's also a graduate of the Otago phys. ed. school and her two brothers, Calvin and Bruce Cochrane, were talented rugby players, Calvin representing Canterbury for a number of years as a loose forward. Raewyn is calm, almost serene, yet forceful and strong and a most competent coach herself, having prepared the Welsh netball team at the World Cup in Jamaica in 2003. Her support for Graham is complete and together they make a tight unit. At times I believe she should be given a Victoria Cross for services above the call of duty.

Will Graham Henry succeed as All Black coach? If he can't, no one can. This is a coach who has been introduced at his peak, a coach who has already experienced the highs and lows that international rugby has to offer, a man who is comfortable in his own skin. But it won't be enough for him to succeed. Henry has always wanted to be the best and he will be aiming to be the best All Black coach ever.

Coaches

The modern coach has to be a motivator, a manipulator, a psychologist, a strategist, a publicist, a public relations exponent to sponsors, a role model, a fitness expert, a leader, a team player, an administrator, a tactician, a technician, an opportunist and a man manager. It's an impossible task. Good administrators have seen this and planned accordingly by limiting the number of functions their coach is required to do.

New Zealand Cricket has gone further by giving the manager the power of a CEO. This was tried by the NZRU at the insistence of John Graham, who had been manager to the Black Caps. The experiment failed when the personalities of manager Andrew Martin and coach John Mitchell clashed. The board backed Mitchell and gave him total power. The rest is history.

The best coach I've seen is Rod Macqueen, the Wallaby coach who guided his nation to World Cup glory in 1999 and won everything and anything worth taking. He did it with humility and dignity and without any of the histrionics that later became the hallmark of England's Clive Woodward.

Macqueen was the ultimate man manager, prepared to delegate but always willing to be accountable for what happened on the field. The series win over the British Lions rivalled the World Cup victory. He was so well organised that he always had time. This was illustrated for me in 1999 before the Bledisloe Cup test in Sydney. Before that game the Aussie media had been dishing it out to the Wallabies and Rod in particular. Just about everyone anticipated that John Hart's All Blacks would thrash the Wallabies.

The New Zealand players were completely off limits to the media for one-on-one interviews from the Wednesday, but I arranged by email to conduct a 30-minute *Deaker Profile* talk with Macqueen on the Thursday. I fully expected him to pull the plug but he arrived at 3.30 p.m., right on time. Sky played the revealing interview immediately before the live telecast of the game. At the end of our conversation I asked Macqueen if I could further impose on him by interviewing him for my seven o'clock radio show. He said he'd have to change his dining arrangements to make that possible.

Only then did I realise that I'd mixed up the time difference between New Zealand and Australia. My show was live at five o'clock Sydney time. Rod grinned and said, 'No problem, mate.' Not only did he manage the radio interview, he took talkback calls until Rod Kafer, who he'd arranged to come on the show, replaced him. The substitute first-five, who would play a highly significant role in the Bledisloe Cup contest, stayed for the full hour.

The Aussies seem to thrive on being the underdogs and react normally and in a relaxed fashion to the pressure. Macqueen's players overwhelmed the All Blacks two days later, a victory that gave them the confidence to go on and win the World Cup.

The other huge advantage the Australians have over New Zealand in sport is that, as a nation, they're more direct, more honest. If they don't like you, they'll call you a prick to your face. In many New Zealand sports the players are more likely to be smarmy to your face, then stick the knife in behind your back.

Steve Rixon, who guided the Black Caps to a new level, graphically illustrated that Aussie directness. Steve had dropped Danny Morrison early in the piece, immediately after he had played a match-saving innings at Eden Park, and I thought the bowler had been given a raw deal. In fact, my objectivity was sorely lacking. Danny had begun to do what too many fast bowlers do towards the end of their careers — he was bowling for tomorrow, holding himself back.

I began to deliver innuendoes on air regarding Steve. Out of the blue, my phone rang. 'Listen, bud, have you got a problem with me?' Rixon barked in his unmistakable Aussie drawl. For once I was short of a word but I eventually spluttered out my reasons. Steve fired back, explaining why he'd dropped Danny, and I was left to like it or lump it. As a result of his directness, Steve and I have become good mates and

I always ring him and try and arrange a get-together when I'm in Sydney. He's flown over on a couple of occasions specifically to appear on my television show.

It was Steve who arranged my prized interview with Steve Waugh. There are few sportsmen I admire more than the gutsy Australian cricket captain, who received a hero's farewell when he announced his retirement at the beginning of 2004. In the interview, done shortly after Waugh had been dropped from the Aussie one-day side, I asked if he would now consider making himself available for New Zealand. 'No way, mate,' was the instant reply.

The structure set up during the Rixon era was a model, indeed a blueprint, for New Zealand sport. Steve's strengths were his positiveness, his ability to get the team to field brilliantly, his mentoring of Adam Parore and his broad appreciation of the game. Other appointments were made to cover his perceived shortcomings. Gilbert Enoka was given the job of goal-setting for individuals, Ashley Ross was responsible for developing individual skills and identifying player weaknesses, often by using video, while John Graham was appointed manager with overall control. Rixon was left to do what he did best, coach. A situation that initially appeared to possess the potential for disaster was turned around through sound administrative logic.

Steve also possesses two other exceptional qualities that top coaches need. He has an eye for talent that was never better illustrated than when he selected Daniel Vettori as a 17-year-old for his national squad. The left-armer is already the most successful spinner this country has produced and very likely will one day captain our test team. Most of all, Rixon is a winner. He's one of the most positive people you could ever encounter, brimful of confidence and with a touch of that Australian arrogance that has made his nation the greatest sporting country in the world.

Jan Cameron also has that quality. As Jan Murphy, she won a silver medal swimming for Australia at the Olympics. Her work with swimmers in this country has been exemplary, training them rigorously, hardening them both physically and mentally. Her methods are based on how she was trained in Australia and now her North Shore club dominates the national championships.

Along with the outstanding Otago coach Duncan Laing, who was Danyon Loader's mentor, Jan has been frustrated by pedantic and largely incompetent swimming administrators. At times she has nearly chucked it in, but her love of the sport and her passion to bring young swimmers to their potential have convinced her to keep trying. She remains frustrated and confused by New Zealand's political correctness, which she thinks has now penetrated fully into the sporting scene. She finds it impossible to accept that this new generation of young Kiwis is prepared to accept second best, doesn't strive to succeed, finds hard work abhorrent and is generally soft, both physically and mentally.

What annoys her more is the acceptance of this attitude by those with the power to make changes. Jan emphasises that there's nothing wrong with the talent base in New Zealand — she believes our athletes are as good as those anywhere in the world; it's the attitude that appals her. (She was brought up with individuals like Dawn Fraser.) So far her pleas have fallen on deaf ears..

Kevin Fallon is a fanatic, totally obsessed with soccer's techniques, skills and structure. I once hid behind a tree at the Mount Maunganui Reserve for an hour and watched Fallon coach three talented young players. Nowhere in the world could they have received finer tuition. Kevin could have been coaching an international side, such was the effort he was putting in. He's forgotten more about football than most other coaches in New Zealand know, yet his expertise was never fully used because he was regarded as a loose cannon. Fiery, unpredictable, at times completely over the top, Kevin Fallon could have been the saviour of the round ball code in New Zealand but instead he's just another casualty.

It's now clear that New Zealand rowing has another Rusty Robertson in coach Richard Tonks. His tuition of Rob Waddell and his work with the Evers-Swindell twins mark him out as a coach of genuine quality. He's a master technician, a coach who gets on with the job in a focused, committed manner. It's not unreasonable to expect that New Zealand will claim rowing medals at the Athens Olympics under his guidance.

Grant Beck helped make New Zealand windsurfing equal to the best in the world. Barbara Kendall is infuriated that Beck is consistently overlooked for the Halberg Awards, claiming that it's a further example of how minor sports are treated. Beck is clearly very hardworking, highly skilled, able to motivate difficult, individualistic windsurfers and completely focused on the job.

Bill Begg, the skating coach who has trained eight skaters to 16 world titles, is scathing about the way minor sports are treated in New Zealand. His coaching resembles Kevin Fallon's in terms of fanaticism. It has to be — he receives little help and hovers on the brink of bankruptcy owing to the amount of time he commits to the sport. Bill looks outside New Zealand for inspiration and isn't frightened to analyse other sports in his determination to identify that extra something that will give his skaters the edge. Bill's biggest problem is his directness, indeed his harshness, in speaking honestly. His confrontation with the Minister of Sport, Trevor Mallard, on my TV show was vintage Begg. I'd love to see Bill given more resources. With his track record, New Zealand could dominate world skating.

Don Tricker is probably the most successful current New Zealand coach. The Black Sox won the world title in softball at East London in South Africa and completed a famous hat trick at Christchurch in 2004. This was a story of Kiwi ingenuity, fortitude and resilience. His players had to pay their own fares to the world championships at East London where they were housed in a school dormitory and quickly discovered that they had room-mates — cockroaches so big and aggressive the boys had to use brooms to fend them off. It was too much for the American team, who checked out after one night. Our blokes turned cockroach hunting into a competitive game. When they weren't hunting roaches with a broom they were competing on the pool table Don had commissioned from somewhere. What was already a tight unit became so cohesive that no other team could touch them. These blokes had already killed hundreds of roaches so they could survive.

Don Tricker is a great man at extolling the Black Sox culture. He constantly refers to their proud history, to the players who have gone before them and to their expectations of each other. Coming first isn't an option, it's an expectation. Tricker commands with a quiet voice, a clear mission, an ability to delegate and a clearly stated policy of accountability.

Tricker is fortunate that most of this had already been established by Mike Walsh, another Wellingtonian, who enjoyed unprecedented success with the men's team and who is now trying to transfer that same culture across to the White Sox, the women's team. If anyone can do it, Mike can.

Ian Ferguson is an icon, the New Zealander who has won the most

When you need a lift, who better to provide it than boxer David Tua, left, and his equally illustrious footballer cousin Inga Tuigamala. The occasion was a golf tournament I helped organise to raise funds for epilepsy awareness. David and Inga won the amateur section and Inga claimed the longest drive (a massive 312 metres).

NORRIE MONTGOMERY

New Zealand sport can claim few better role models than Sir Bob Charles who, incredibly, has been achieving at the highest level for half a century. It's always a privilege to have him as a guest on my radio programme.

No prizes for identifying the most talented golfer in this foursome. Yes, it's Sir Bob Charles. His playing partners in a pro-am tournament at Gulf Harbour are, from left, Richard Kahn, my regular partner at Gulf Harbour, Neil Berryman, the general manager of finance and administration at Harvey Norman, and yours truly.

At the time of rugby's first World Cup in 1987, he was the greatest loose forward in the game. Sixteen years on, at the time of this radio interview, Michael Jones was assistant coach of Manu Samoa as they prepared for the World Cup in Australia. DEAKER COLLECTION

Regency Duty Free's CEO Kelvin Ricketts, left, a supporter of my radio programme for more than a decade, with New Zealand's world youth triathlon champion Terenza Bozzone, who has benefited from the Regency Duty Free Sports Foundation. DEAKER COLLECTION

Where better to interview Michael Campbell, a likeable extrovert, than on a golf course, after playing a few holes together. Here we are at Kauri Cliffs, New Zealand's most scenic golf course. DEAKER COLLECTION

We don't usually encourage such close fraternisation with our *Deaker on Sport* guests, but my wife Sharon found the dishy former British Lions captain Gavin Hastings irresistible. DEAKER COLLECTION

A pretty special address in Omakau, Central Otago — Deaker St, named after my father, who was the headmaster at Omakau School for 16 years.

Many of my broadcasts are done at outside venues. This one was at the Avillion Hotel in Sydney during the Rugby World Cup.

Martin Snedden, who has set the standard for sports administration in New Zealand, in a relaxed mood in the Deaker den. He's on my right with his wife Annie on the extreme left. The others, from left, are my son John, daughter Kate and wife Sharon.

Hamming it up at a function at *Sky City* with Peter Leitch, a.k.a. The Mad Butcher, who is the official ambassador for New Zealand League. More importantly, he's a good mate.

Weet-Bix Tryathlons annually cater for 15,000 children throughout New Zealand. This is one of my favourite photos, placing a winner's badge around a delighted young competitor.

gold medals. During his heyday as a kayaker, the sport enjoyed un-precedented success and popularity. When he retired, along with Paul MacDonald and Alan Thompson, kayaking lost its impetus. Now 'Ferg' is back and the results are there for all to see. Ben Fouhy won gold at the 2003 world championship and, together with Ian's son Steven, quali-fied in the K2 category for the Athens Olympics.

Ian brings to coaching the same focus, energy and diligence he brought to competition. He believes ardently in the ability of his team and consistently sets them fresh, tougher goals. Like all good coaches, Ferguson is intensely loyal to his boys, often talking up their chances in public in front of them. You can almost see the paddlers thinking, 'Well, if Ferg thinks we can win, we obviously can.' Few top former competitors make the transition to coaching as successfully as Ian Ferguson.

Yvonne Willering got a raw deal when she was dropped from the position of coach of the Silver Ferns. She and Southlander Robyn Broughton were a combination that would have won the World Cup against an ageing Australian line-up well past its best. Broughton's recent record with the Southern Sting and Verdon College stamped her as the most successful coach in the sport. She's a brilliant motiva-tor, a diligent strategist, a shrewd competitor and a wonderful woman. Her teams love her.

However, Netball New Zealand decided a change was needed and appointed Ruth Aitken, which turned out to be an inspired decision: she guided the team to World Cup glory in Jamaica. Ruth is quiet, con-trolled and calm but has a certain presence about her. She never panics, regardless of the circumstances.

I can claim first-hand experience of her gentle demeanour because we taught together at Takapuna Grammar School. On one occasion I needed a witness for a caning. Normally, I would have asked another man, but I couldn't find a male teacher anywhere, so I asked Ruth to witness the caning. Later, she calmly took me aside and said, 'Murray, never ask me to do that again. I found it sickening.'

Chris and Mark Lewis are starting to develop some promising ten-nis players, none with greater potential than Marina Erakovic. Chris, who was a Wimbledon finalist overcome only by the great John McEnroe, has a firm philosophy of setting goals as high as possible and getting young people to work strenuously towards these. He's a libertarian who believes in fostering the skills of the individual. If we're to produce another champion there's no doubt that he or she will come out of the Lewis camp.

Daniel Anderson has enjoyed more success with the Warriors than any of his predecessors. Frank Endacott was hamstrung by an incompetent board and the criticisms of Graham Lowe, who seems to have a personal agenda to make life as difficult as possible for any New Zealand coach who challenges his record. Frank told me that after he won the New Zealand appointment two former coaches rang to wish him well and warn him about Lowe.

Anderson guided the Warriors through to the NRL Grand Final in 2002 and into the semifinals in 2003. Given that the team had consistently underperformed over a long time, this represented an outstanding achievement. A former schoolteacher, Anderson is studious in his preparation, thorough in his technique and has quickly developed a strong relationship with the Polynesian players who make up the bulk of the team, something John Monie never managed.

I've known Laurie Mains almost all my life. We went to school together, played for the Southern Rugby Club from schoolboys through to seniors and even featured in the same Otago team. We've discussed, debated, argued, fought and at times even agreed on different aspects of rugby for almost 50 years.

What I admire most about Laurie is his work ethic. This was the quality, more than anything, that made him an All Black and a fine coach. When others were wanting to give up he was just getting started. He's been accused of being manipulative, authoritative, one-eyed and excessively competitive. So what! Much the same could be levelled at other outstandingly successful coaches like Fred Allen, Vic Cavanagh, Eric Watson and Dick Everest.

Laurie was a product of his environment and the eras in which he functioned. No one has been more committed to the Southern Club and Otago. His most outspoken critics, Otago CEO John Hornbrook and former Otago and New Zealand captain Anton Oliver, seem to have conveniently forgotten that Laurie coached for nothing for 20 years before the game went professional.

Sean Fitzpatrick has said on a number of occasions that Mains is the best forward coach he ever had. Given that Fitzpatrick was the best All Black forward of his era, it's hard to imagine a bigger rap.

Robin Brooke is another who says that, when it came to forward play, Laurie was out on his own. There's little doubt that had Mains' All Blacks not suffered food poisoning 48 hours before the World Cup final in 1995 they would have won the title.

Mains was probably a better coach after that World Cup experience. No other All Black coach came remotely near to bringing the best out of Jonah Lomu. Mains used him as an unstoppable missile out wide, declining to sacrifice him as a battering ram, as many others did. Throughout his career Mains prided himself on being a players' coach. He put them first and was fearlessly prepared to fight their battles with authorities and the media.

Tragically, in his final year of coaching Laurie's methods came under fire from some of the underachieving Otago players and Hornbrook, who somehow managed to draw a comparison between the atmosphere in the Highlanders Super-12 squad and Dachau concentration camp. Although little was made public, it appears that Mains successfully won an out-of-court settlement over those explosive comments and Hornbrook was replaced as Otago CEO.

Mains would have taken little satisfaction from such events. He only ever wanted the best for his team. In terms of longevity, he rivals North Auckland's Ted Griffin as the longest-surviving New Zealand provincial rugby coach. Sadly, it looks as though Mains is now lost to New Zealand rugby. He would be an ideal chairman of selectors for the All Blacks, but all his experience and expertise have been sacrificed in the wake of one of the ugliest and most unfortunate chapters in the history of Otago rugby.

Tab Baldwin has endeared himself to New Zealand sports followers. Fluent, intense, sincere and shrewd, he has a wonderful background in the sport he loves. His father was a basketball coach for over 40 years and Tab has been greatly influenced by him. After a mixed start to his coaching career in Otago, he enjoyed numerous championship successes with Auckland, a team that had underachieved for decades. Just when he was becoming overanxious about his chances of ever coaching the Tall Blacks, Tab was given the job. He was instantly successful and has taken the team to heights followers of the sport in this country never thought possible. Beating Australia was handsome enough, we thought; finishing fourth at the world championships, ahead of the United States, bordered on the unbelievable!

No one works harder than Tab at analysing opposition play to develop an effective game plan. Often during the world championships, he worked through the night, assessing videos and strategising. He handles the media with aplomb and treats those of us with limited technical appreciation of the game with dignity.

Gordon Tietjens is a most remarkable coach and selector. He has to be to cope with the restrictions placed on him when he selects his New Zealand sevens squads. Super-12 squads and, of course, New Zealand selections take precedence over his sevens team, which means he's forever developing fresh talent. He scours divisions two and three and even checks out school teams and inevitably uncovers exciting new players.

His continued success on the world championship circuit, not to mention the Hong Kong, Commonwealth Games and World Cup titles his teams have taken out, stamp him as one of New Zealand sport's most successful sports coaches. His achievements are matched only by his reputation as a ruthless trainer. Jonah Lomu was never fitter than when Titch was pushing his buttons. Certainly no coach presents his players fitter. I hope he'll soon be given a Super-12 team so he can demonstrate that his coaching talents aren't confined to the seven-a-side arena.

It's rare, indeed, probably unprecedented, for a young coach to resign with his team in possession of both the Ranfurly Shield and the Air New Zealand NPC title, but that's what Wayne Pivac did at the conclusion of the 2003 season. He demonstrated an ability to compromise and to surround himself with quality fellow coaches, qualities too often found lacking in both sport and business in New Zealand.

Graham Henry had been enormously successful with Auckland, and the Blues, prior to his departure for Wales and when he returned ahead of schedule public conjecture ran rampant as to whether he would be allocated a meaningful position in Auckland rugby. Pivac came under pressure not to involve Henry. Even the All Black coach John Mitchell suggested that such an appointment would be unwise. Pivac ignored the advice and Auckland rugby flourished with Pivac, Grant Fox and Henry collectively in charge. Their squad was decimated when the All Blacks headed for the World Cup but they developed an exciting new line-up that blew away Canterbury at Jade Stadium, Otago at Carisbrook and Wellington at the Cake Tin with rugby of breathtaking quality. Pivac was deservedly named coach of the year at the 2003 Steinlager Awards dinner and his new challenge is as coach of Fiji. He's bound to make an impact there too.

Kirsten Hellier has had remarkable success as coach of the young thrower Valerie Adams. She's completely dedicated to her charge and took Adams into her house after Valerie lost her mother. Hillier is a believer in setting clear, achievable goals and brings to her coaching an intensity and focus that marked the work of the great Arthur Lydiard.

It's surprising that New Zealand produces so many quality coaches, given the way we treat them. We have almost no courses for coaches, no diplomas or degrees, no instruction manuals and almost no pool of experience. New Zealand needs resources for coaches, which should include everything available from overseas in the form of literature, videos, scientific information, nutritional advice, medical findings, psychological data and motivational aids. Obviously the body to set this up is SPARC (Sport and Recreation New Zealand), which has the necessary financial capacity. If it isn't prepared to establish a degree or diploma course, it could at least foster seminar programmes.

Imagine a seminar with overseas experts like Rod Macqueen, Wayne Bennett, Sir Alex Ferguson, Jill McIntosh and Phil Jackson giving presentations on motivation, leadership, decision making, developing strategies, video analysis, fitness, delegation, the role of the assistant coach, the relationship with the manager and all the other areas that must be in sync for a coach to operate at optimum level.

Within the various sports, and particularly rugby, there doesn't appear to be any training or promotion structure for coaches. They're left to sink or swim on their results, so that when there's a fluctuation in form the coach's future is thrown into jeopardy. No wonder most of our coaches appear to be more interested in short-term gain than long-term goals. Most of the people who appoint coaches are ill-qualified to do so. Many recent NZRU appointments followed recommendations from a company of personnel consultants who often used female representatives to narrow down the candidates. There are similarities between coaching at top level and a senior executive position in business but there remains one key difference: senior executives can switch from company to company but coaches are restricted to their specialist sport.

A coach's most important quality must be knowledge of the game.

Without it, no one can coach to the top level and that knowledge can be accumulated only through years of experience. I'm a firm believer in the idea that a coach must serve his apprenticeship.

Graham Henry is a classic example. He cut his teeth with the Auckland Grammar First XV before moving on to the New Zealand schools team and Auckland Colts. From there he coached Auckland to NPC and Ranfurly Shield success and the Blues to two Super 12 titles. The final step was on to the international stage with Wales and the British Lions. What better preparation could there be for an All Black coach? Too often we appoint individuals who are seriously short on experience, there being no better example than John Mitchell.

New Zealand needs an institute of coaching. Every university and technical institute in the country seems to have a sports administration diploma on offer but none offers an in-depth coaching course. Such a course combined with practical experience would provide a coaching pool that is sadly depleted at the moment. We delight in throwing coaches on to the scrapheap when their time is up.

What use has been made of the Arthur Lydiards, the Rusty Robertsons, the Arch Jelleys, the Fred Allens and other giants of the past? Precious little, I suggest. All that knowledge, all that experience and, in most cases, all that desire to help has been ignored.

Administrators

No New Zealand sport has been better served by its administrators in modern times than cricket. It started with the appointment of Chris Doig, MA, expert English teacher and opera singer, as CEO.

In just two short years Doig had transformed Wellington's biennial arts festival, now the New Zealand International Arts Festival, which was floundering around with debts of a million dollars, into a vibrant, profit-making event. His appointment to cricket's top job was treated with scepticism by many in the press. Strange that, because academically he was better qualified than those who were writing about him. He was so articulate and fluent that most of them probably failed to understand him.

Perhaps he was wrong in his handling of the Glenn Turner affair but he could justify his decision by showing that under Turner's successor, Australian Steve Rixon, the Black Caps became more successful. In fact, they hadn't enjoyed such success since the days of (Sir) Richard Hadlee, Geoff Howarth, Ian Smith, John Wright, Bruce Edgar and co. Thanks to Doig, Chris Cairns' international career was revived while Stephen Fleming has gone on to become our most successful test captain of all time. Any judgment of an administrator should be based on what he leaves behind, and in this respect Doig was superb.

He headhunted the former New Zealand medium pace bowler Martin Snedden to succeed him, first revealing his intentions, interestingly enough, at the function after my inaugural *Deaker on Sport* television show in 2000. Doig and former New Zealand test fast bowler Bob Cunis were my guests for the evening and all my sponsors were there. But that didn't stop Doig, who had Snedden firmly in his sights and declared that the CEO's job was his if he wanted it.

Doig had been shabbily treated by Team New Zealand. Their boss Ralph Norris had invited him for an interview when they were seeking a replacement for Sir Peter Blake and Doig's account of what took place shows clearly why Team New Zealand failed so appallingly.

The interview was a disaster. Doig arrived on time to find Norris the only trustee there. Peter Menzies arrived about 15 minutes later but spent the entire interview either ducking in or out of the room or talking unnecessarily on his cellphone. It's hard to believe that Menzies, a director of Mainzeal, could be so unprofessional and rude. Tom Schnackenberg showed up 30 minutes late and sloped into the room. In Doig's opinion, they weren't remotely interested in him. Presumably, Menzies and Schnackenberg had already decided that Ross Blackman was the man for them and they were annoyed with Norris for thrusting Doig on them. Whatever the real scenario, Doig was shattered by the treatment he received, and that's not easily done, given his natural exuberance and vitality.

Martin Snedden was fortunate to inherit a game in good shape, administratively. A well-established and successful commercial programme was in place, securing New Zealand Cricket's financial position well into the future. Doig had also handed over to him an outstanding High Performance programme with a near new academy at Lincoln College. Doig was the innovator, the entrepreneur whose energy, enthusiasm and foresight had laid a superb development plan with the infrastructure already in place. With his more advanced cricket knowledge Snedden has been able to develop this into what is arguably the finest cricket administration in the world.

The transition between Doig and Snedden was seamless. Doig was the right man for his time. Snedden is the right man now. It's a mark of Doig's intelligence and vision that he headhunted a person with contrasting talents to take the organisation to the new level.

I had mixed feelings about Snedden quitting Auckland and the law. He remains one of my closest friends, a man of the highest principles and values. He'd been my solicitor for more than a decade and as a trustee his name features on every piece of land I own.

Previously, I'd been the client of one of New Zealand's largest firms of solicitors, until the day I visited their new office block. It was lavish, furnished with all the mod cons and boasting a reception desk staffed by private school girls speaking a version of English more appropriate in the West End of London than in downtown Auckland. When I asked for my files one of the junior partners came out to enquire why. I had no difficulty supplying the answer: 'Listen, mate, someone's got to pay for this joint with its inch-thick carpet, and it won't be me.'

I carried the file down the road to Vulcan Lane where I knew Snedden had his office. The lift didn't work and the linoleum looked as though it had been rescued from a Chinese takeaway but Snedden proved to be an outstanding lawyer, efficient, effective, painstaking and reasonable. His dress sense even then was more suited to a warehouse worker or woodwork teacher. I'm sure he didn't own a sports coat and his ties were patently freebies from cricket testimonials. But his advice was superb, always direct, logical and objective.

No wonder he's set the standard for sports administrators in New Zealand. In fact, he's taken it to a new level. In simple terms, he knows his business and despite his passion for the game he remains objective, hard-working and utterly professional. He is also surrounding himself with quality individuals: the appointments of John Bracewell and Lindsay Crocker are prime examples.

His highly publicised battle with Rob Nichol and the New Zealand Cricket Players' Association was vintage Snedden as he fought tooth and nail against a competent if somewhat inexperienced adversary, running rings around Nichol, particularly in the public arena. But Nichol is no fool and the experience has undoubtedly left him wiser, stronger and more conciliatory. (He demonstrated this a year later when he successfully negotiated an extremely good bonus for the All Blacks had they won the World Cup.) Nichol will prove to be an important figure in the future development of professional sport in this country. In his favour is that he won't come up against a more gifted sports communicator.

If Snedden is light years ahead of any other sports CEO in New Zealand, until recent times I would have classified Warriors CEO Mick Watson as the second best. He may still be. Watson owes his current employment to one of New Zealand's more unusual and individual characters, Matthew Ridge.

They first encountered each other when Watson was with Pepsi, the major sponsor of the Manly Sea Eagles during the time when Ridgey was at his peak as a footballer, kicking goals like Jonny Wilkinson and fearlessly tackling opponents.

The way Watson tells the story, Ridgey was having his salary topped up for making occasional promotional appearances for Pepsi. When Ridgey's appearances became less than occasional, Watson put his foot down and demanded he justify the extra cash. Mutual respect was established and a working relationship was struck. Consequently, when new Warriors owner Eric Watson invited Ridge to help create the new club, Mick Watson was at the top of his hit list.

My first encounter with Watson was at Seamart Restaurant, shortly after his appointment. The Mad Butcher set up the meeting and it's fair to say neither the Butcher nor I could get a word in. Watson was obviously nervous and chattered away incessantly. I wasn't impressed.

Watson appointed Daniel Anderson as coach and the pair turned the struggling Warriors around, although Watson remains an enigma. He still talks too much and tends to make promises he can't keep. Yet he works hard, is full of good intentions and has more vision than many other New Zealand administrators. He can be charming, delightful and personable, full of objectivity and common sense. He can also be rude, pigheaded, subjective and irrational.

He exposed his worst side in 2003, after promising me a closer working relationship with the Warriors. I didn't request it, but the Mad Butcher and Terry Baker, the Warriors' stats man, who were both at the meeting when Watson made this promise, said it would be interesting to see if it came to pass. It hasn't, because Watson has little, if any, control over coach Anderson.

For a reason I've never sorted out, Anderson doesn't like me. (The Mad Butcher reckons John Mitchell got to Anderson and put him right off me.) Fair enough, it's not all one-sided. I find him boring, colourless and reserved, hardly the ideal profile for television or radio interviews. Nevertheless, I've requested half a dozen interviews with him, all of which have been declined. The Warriors must be an unusual organisation for the CEO to allow his coach to adopt this attitude. After all, my programmes are the only ones syndicated nationwide on both Radio Sport and Newstalk ZB while my television show *Deaker on Sport*, which screens at 8.30 p.m. every Monday, is the only sports show in New Zealand to feature the presenter's name in the title.

I've searched back through the tapes to see if, or when, I said anything remotely derogatory about Daniel Anderson, but to no avail. Frankly, I've requested my last interview with him. When I raised the issue with Watson he was nothing short of insulting. He suggested I approach Daniel and sort it out. On a much more important issue Watson failed. For some crazy reason he released Ivan Cleary and Kevin Campion from their contracts with the Warriors. One was a deadly accurate goalkicker, equal to the best in the NRL, the other a team leader in everything except title. Neither has been adequately replaced and they have been sorely missed. Cleary made it patently clear he wanted to stay and was prepared to do so for a smaller salary. This revelation was made on *Deaker on Sport* and remains in our archive footage, although Watson still denies it.

Watson remains an administrator of considerable potential, though he's not half as smart as he thinks he is. But he's still light years ahead of a couple of his predecessors, Ian Robson, who became the darling of league's sycophantic media in the Warriors' formative years, and Trevor McKewen, whom I would rate as the worst sports administrator I've dealt with. Perhaps that's because he ended up in a job he'd never been trained for, having a background in journalism. But Watson needs someone to rope him in, someone to advise him, someone to confide in, someone to remind him that his job is controlling a rugby league club.

On the other hand, the chief executive of the NZRU, Chris Moller, grows in stature daily. He's conciliatory, honest and uncomplicated. Most important of all, he arrives without baggage. Chris would be the first to acknowledge his lack of rugby knowledge but he's prepared to hand the rugby management over to Steve Tew.

Unlike Watson, Moller delivers. John Mitchell had a major problem with me because I bagged him mercilessly on my show for his continued selection of Reuben Thorne, his non-selection of Christian Cullen and his general demeanour. Moller rang me to arrange an interview, even travelling to Auckland to discuss my relationship with Mitchell. Subsequently, Mitchell appeared on my television show and I wrote him a letter of apology for an article of mine that appeared in a World Cup booklet.

Moller was in the unfortunate position of succeeding David Rutherford, a man painfully out of his depth. Rutherford was so inept that he simply couldn't front the media when it was his duty to do so. Soon after his appointment I contacted the NZRU's media person, Jackie Maitland, requesting an interview. She replied that David had said that because I had a reputation as the hardest interviewer around, he didn't want to confront me for at least three months.

All I wanted was a soft interview, I assured her. You know, questions like, 'Who is David Rutherford and why did he want the job?'

'No,' said Maitland, 'David doesn't want hard questions like that.'

Fortunately, both Rutherford and Maitland have moved on. Moller, on his performance to date, could become a good CEO.

Steve Tew performed outstandingly while CEO at Canterbury. He's certainly forthright to the point of being blunt, even arrogant. Some people go further and even suggest he's a bully. If he is, he certainly selects his targets carefully. Tew's biggest error of judgment was to ask me to become a referee for him when David Rutherford was appointed CEO. The way NZRU board members look at me, I would have thought having Murray Deaker on your list of referees was tantamount to announcing you're unquestionably too hard to control. A couple of years ago, one person being interviewed by the NZRU was asked, 'How would you deal with difficult members of the media? Take Murray Deaker, for example, he's impossible.' High praise, indeed.

At the Crusaders, Tew helped to set the standard for all franchises in the Super 12. The red and blacks quickly became professional, decisive and innovative and bounded clear of the other franchises. The 2004 season is a crucial one for Tew, the one survivor of the loss of the Rugby World Cup sub-hosting rights. Many believe he should have been sacked. He must be seen to be a national administrator now, not a servant of the red and blacks.

If anyone doubts the impact a CEO can have on a professional sports team, they need look no further than the Blues. Auckland rugby had been well served for years by Link Warren, who used to run the entire show with a couple of part-time secretaries, a far cry from today's ever expanding bureaucracy. He was succeeded by Murray Wright and later Peter Scutts, both competent administrators of differing strengths. Wright loved rugby and had a rich background in it. Scutts knew less about the game but also recognised his own limitations. He was entirely willing to give Graham Henry a free hand as coach while he expertly attracted fresh sponsors. Throughout the '80s and early '90s Auckland and the Blues continued to prosper.

But then came Geoff Hipkins and disaster. Personally, I've nothing against the man. In fact, after I'd successfully led the public battle to have the famous blue and white jersey reinstated, Geoff presented me with a personalised one inscribed 'Deaks'. The only others to receive their own jerseys that day were the knights, 'Willie' and 'TPs', Sir Wilson Whineray and Sir Terry McLean. Rarely had I been included in such illustrious company; I'll always value that jersey. Beyond that, though, Mr Hipkins appears to have pleased no one. In fact, it's not too strong to suggest he was universally detested by his staff and the sponsors.

On one memorable occasion he smashed a heavy menu board over the head of Peter Wills, of DB Breweries, who remain Auckland's major sponsor. It was a very public assault on an individual who'd established a significant rapport with both staff and players at Auckland rugby.

Roger Whatman, who had represented Auckland with distinction at fullback, was working as a coaching coordinator for the ARU at the time. He telephoned me to ask for a private meeting during which he revealed the state of near anarchy that existed among the coaching and administration staff. The way Roger told it, Hipkins had insulted and upset so many people at a staff Christmas party there was a queue lining up to drop him.

Perhaps the real blame should be levelled at the board that appoints such people. In the *New Zealand Herald* column I was writing at the time, I named the board. The chairman at the time, Rodger Fisher, was furious. Perhaps he felt his decisions shouldn't be questioned. Certainly, my experience of sporting boards in this country is that the individuals who comprise them are keen on the perks but most reluctant to accept any responsibility when things go wrong. The Auckland board of that time not only appointed the CEO but also turned a blind eye to his behaviour and to the subsequent chaos. Theirs was the ultimate responsibility.

Bill McGowan has to be New Zealand's unluckiest administrator. When he took over the Warriors from Ian Robson, McGowan made real inroads into turning the struggling franchise around. He's hardworking, diligent and logical, and quickly established a sound working relationship with coach Frank Endacott, who is a man of integrity and honesty.

They were unquestionably on the right track, until along came

Graham Lowe, Malcolm Boyle, Jeff Green and Tainui. What followed, in my opinion, marked the low point in New Zealand sports administration, no small statement given some of the blockheads who, over the years, have dared to call themselves administrators.

Graham Lowe was one of the best coaches league has produced but then he became one of the worst administrators. His problem is that he can't bear to share centre stage with anyone. In my opinion, his time at the Warriors was horrendous. He made one massive mistake after another. The worst was to appoint journeyman journalist Trevor McKewen as his CEO. Another was the very public falling-out with his former close friend and Warrior coach, Mark Graham.

Trevor had operated as PR agent for Super League during the battle that almost finished the grand old game. Not without intelligence, McKewen soon found that, as CEO of the Warriors, he was in effect the modern-day James Busby, a man with a title but no power.

'Lowey' couldn't help himself. He interfered in finance, in selection, in coaching and in marketing. He thought he knew it all, but in fact he knew nothing. Trevor quickly became surplus to requirements, the CEO of nothing. I doubt if he was even given the authority to purchase the oranges for halftime.

Lowe appointed one of the game's legends, Mark Graham, to coach the team. They soon fell out though, first privately, then publicly. Graham was given none of the authority or independence he needed to make a success of the job.

Meanwhile, as owners of the Warriors, Tainui was losing money hand over fist. Leighton Smith, a genuine league fan, and I were summoned by senior Tainui members to discuss the club's shambles at a private meeting at the Heritage Hotel in Auckland. The Tainui elders outlined a story of gross mismanagement and gave authority for me to reveal all on my Newstalk ZB programme the following evening. Two hours before the show went to air, and after I had prepared my script, they pulled the plug, on the advice of one Michael Stiassny, an accountant specialising in bankruptcy and winding up financially unsound organisations.

I've never met Mr Stiassny but he has a reputation for being ruthless and tough. In my opinion, his advice to Tainui was highly questionable. By not revealing the manner in which they'd been misled, they were instead left looking ridiculous, and the truth was effectively hidden from the public. As far as I'm concerned, the Warriors needed Lowe, McKewen and Stiassny like Bill English needed Maurice Williamson.

At the time, I believed the Warriors were fated to head in the same direction as the *Rainbow Warrior*, straight to the bottom. The sad saga represented the nadir in modern New Zealand sports administration, challenged only by Murray McCaw and David Rutherford's effort over the 2003 Rugby World Cup.

Of the other sports, golf was a shining beacon — until 2004 when national coach Mel Tongue had a serious falling-out with New Zealand Golf. Under the late Grant Clements, a blueprint was developed that helped New Zealand win the Eisenhower Cup in 1992. Philip Tataurangi, Michael Campbell, Stephen Scahill and Grant Moorhead may have held the clubs but the shotmaker was Grant Clements. Quiet, unassuming, thoughtful and profound, Clements was an administrator who set standards that have ensured the successful future of the sport in our country.

Netball's Shelley McMeeken made a huge call in dumping Yvonne Willering and Robyn Broughton, the two most successful provincial coaches this country has seen. Yet it all paid off at the World Cup in Jamaica: under Ruth Aitken, we took the title, justifying McMeeken's actions.

Kerry Clarke is a bright, enthusiastic boss of bowls in New Zealand, prepared to make innovative changes to bring his sport into the 21st century. It isn't easy for him because there are elements in bowls administration that would make the papacy appear trendy. Despite them, Clarke has pushed through coloured clothing, coloured bowls for television coverage and fully integrated women into the game. Together with Gary Sutcliffe he has worked hard to attract younger people to the game. He's prepared to use good people like Stu Scott, an animated commentator, to increase the profile of bowls.

Ramesh Patel of hockey fame and Mike Stanley of rowing are two administrators who have served their sports well. Both men are hardworking, earnest professionals who have extensive knowledge of their codes from having been top competitors themselves. It isn't essential to have such a background but when it's combined with qualities such as honesty, sincerity and diligence, it gives an administrator an edge.

Chris Turner is a tragic figure, though he would be the last person to describe himself in that way. Nor would he welcome any sympathy.

No one has expended such vast reserves of time, money and energy for so little return as Turner with his beloved Kingz. His sole gains have been heartaches, worries and condemnation. From day one, he has been torn to shreds by the *New Zealand Herald* soccer writer Terry Maddaford, yet Turner continues to allow Maddaford to interview him. Anyone else would have told Maddaford where to stick his notepad, biro and computer a long time ago. Turner is the ultimate optimist, always seeing the half of the glass that's full. Sadly, he is now the main problem at the Kingz. In the way Taine Randell became associated with All Black failures and exhausted his catalogue of losing speeches in 1998, Turner is seen now as the boss of a bunch of losers. He should usher himself quietly out the back door.

The sport that's suffered most from shocking administration in New Zealand is tennis. It's been in decline for many, many years; indeed, without the work of the Lewis Brothers, Chris and Mark, the sport would almost expire. There's something radically wrong with the set-up, but it gives the impression it doesn't want to address the problem. Tennis in New Zealand is an embarrassment, administered by people who are content for it to remain stationary while they retain their tip-top jobs. Pat O'Rourke should have made a difference during his time as CEO because he's efficient and ambitious, yet he was unable to spark the sport into action.

It will be interesting to see if Don Turner, the latest CEO, can make an impact. He has a background in tennis and comes from an impressive business background. I suspect he is fighting an uphill battle though.

Graham Pearce and Richard Palmer both run highly successful professional tournaments in Auckland during the Christmas holiday period, but that isn't enough to bolster the sport nationally. Frankly, I'm sick of watching Kiwis who have been given wild cards get knocked out in the first round, while both tournaments are dominated by players whose names defy pronunciation.

The remaining sports are much of a muchness — amateur bodies run by amateurs without vision or foresight. Swimming is a case in point. Two outstanding swim coaches, Duncan Laing and Jan Cameron, spend far too much of their time fighting and arguing with the national body, instead of being allocated the space, time and independence to get on with their jobs.

And what about SPARC? The average Kiwi would scarcely know such an organisation existed. It replaced the Hillary Commission and the New Zealand Sports Foundation. Although SPARC is headed by an intelligent man, Nick Hill, he's out of his depth because he simply doesn't have the sporting background, or the natural empathy with sport, to do the job justice and is poorly equipped to make decisions. With the notable exception of Don Tricker, the highly successful coach of the Black Sox, he appears to have surrounded himself with Wellington Wallies, bureaucrats who are as useless as tits on a bull. Sir Ron Scott, Sir Brian Lochore and Sir Wilson Whineray, the three former heads of the Hillary Commission, were all charismatic personalities, which Hill is not.

His early initiative in identifying seven key sports for funding was stupid and ill-advised; in fact, it was so inane, I doubt SPARC will ever recover from it. John Graham, who headed the inquiry into New Zealand sport, rightly feels betrayed and disillusioned.

Part of SPARC's considerable funding goes to the local sports bodies, such as Sport Otago, Sport Auckland, Sport North Harbour and so on. These organisations vary widely from the good to the atrocious and SPARC seems incapable of bringing the bad ones into line. Unless SPARC gets its act together, it should be folded. It has squandered enough taxpayer money and is serving little or no purpose. In the United States, the home of professional sport, the cliché for success is, 'If the front desk isn't operating efficiently, the team will lose.' Sadly, we haven't learnt that lesson in most New Zealand sports.

The real problem lies with the people who make up the boards. Too often they're colourless characters, completely lacking in charisma and decision-making ability, frightened to stir the pot and desperate to preserve their perks. The last thing they believe in is accountability or responsibility. Many of them also sit on the boards of national companies, so it becomes apparent why we tolerate inefficiency and incompetence in New Zealand business. It's their dishonesty and fervent belief in secrecy that hold back this country much more than any trade union official or lazy employee. They fear transparency because that would expose them for what they are — phoneys. Until this old-boy network is ripped down New Zealand sport will achieve only limited goals and New Zealand society will continue to tread water.

Golf

Golf is like marriage: if you want to succeed you need to work at it. If you don't deal with the details, things will come crashing down around your ears. And also, as with marriage, you have your good days and bad days. Both these institutions demand complete commitment, total dedication and constant adherence to the basics. It's impossible to say which is the more challenging, but both can be fun, exciting and fulfilling while at the same time frustrating and challenging. Certainly, neither is ever boring.

Sadly, I didn't start playing golf seriously until I was in my early fifties. Like anyone who had played cricket to a reasonable level, I found I was able to quickly reduce my handicap to 24 — then the fun started.

My first introduction to serious golf happened when Richard Ellis, the golf manager at Gulf Harbour, invited me to play in the pro-am that preceded the World Cup of Golf in 1998. Sharon was invited to be my caddy. I should have known I was in trouble when her sole response was, 'Wonderful, dear. What do I wear? Should I buy a new outfit?'

Richard coupled me up with the Scottish representatives Colin Montgomery and Andrew Coultard. I didn't know Coultard at all but Monty had a reputation as a difficult bastard, intolerant of those who don't understand the game.

Sharon's natural exuberance had disappeared completely by the time we arrived at the first tee. She had coped all right with me being interviewed by TVNZ and radio but the sight of more than 1000 spectators overwhelmed her. She was wearing a spotless white T-shirt and when I asked for the first club, the colour of her face matched that of her top.

She handed me a putter. It was understandable she should be confused. After all, I'd bought her a set of clubs the previous week that didn't have a putter. When I drew this to her attention, she replied, 'It's all right, there's one here with a P on it,' and proudly pulled out the pitching wedge. As I was lining up my tee shot, the awful thought entered my head that I might have an air shot. Fortunately, I whacked the ball down the middle and ended up bogeying the first hole.

The second at Gulf Harbour is a long par five, up a hill. I got away a reasonable drive and was walking up the hill with Monty, talking rugby, when suddenly my caddy said, 'Look, darling, this is silly. I've only got short legs and you and Colin have long ones. If you pull the cart up the hill, I'll push it down the other side.' Monty reckoned it was the only time in his golfing career he saw a caddy quit after just one and a half holes.

You should take people the way you find them. I found Colin Montgomery to be a complete gentleman, interested in and knowledgeable about the All Blacks and keen to help with golf tips. And Andrew Coultard was a total delight, full of good humour and equally eager to assist. A couple of days later, when they were right into the business of trying to win the World Cup for Scotland, Monty had a shocker, by his high standards. Sharon, who was helping with the production of my programme, was totally nonplussed when Colin brushed past her and wouldn't accede to an interview with 'my Murray'. It didn't stop her going to Andrew and saying, 'Colin's being unreasonable so you'll have to do the interview.' It's a mark of Coultard's chivalry that he acquiesced.

Nick Faldo and his partner won the cup for England. Plainly, there's no love lost between Nick and Monty because the Scot was not impressed with Faldo's dark glasses. 'The bloody game is hard enough,' he commented, 'without looking at the ball as though it's the middle of the night.'

Gulf Harbour is my favourite course and I try to play it at least weekly. Mostly, I play with Richard Kahn, a club member. We met in casual circumstances on the course when I was on a 15-handicap and he was on a 7 — I'm now on an 8 and he's on 2, so we've put in a fair bit of time together. There's a major advantage in playing regularly with someone who's better than you: not only does it lift your game but also you don't have to go hunting for the ball.

My most satisfying victory was to beat my old sparring partner from radio, Larry Williams. Larry is the worst-tempered golfer ever to throw a club, and he throws plenty. For years, the banter between us was animated. I lost count of the number of times strangers came up and asked, 'Who's the better golfer, you or Larry?' The shoot-out was arranged for Gulf Harbour, to be televised by Philip Leishman for his *Golf Show* on Sky. I was allowed to select two holes, Larry one. Obviously, I chose the fourth and the 10th, holes that gave me a one-shot advantage on handicap.

My first tee shot was a shocker, barely making it to the women's tee, but fortunately Sky's camera failed and I had to replay it. At my second attempt, I made a birdie while Larry won the 10th and we advanced to the 15th, a par three surrounded by bunkers, all square. My ball finished 5 metres from the hole while Larry smacked his into the bunker under the hole and took eight to get out. I was laughing so much it took me three putts to get down. So when I'm asked now who the better golfer is, I simply say, 'Didn't you see the shoot-out on TV?'

When it was announced that Tiger Woods was coming to the New Zealand Open at Paraparaumu, I was like a kid waiting for Christmas. After all, Tiger was the number one figure in the world of sport, an icon matched only by Muhammed Ali, Michael Jordan and Pele. His status was beyond question. Few, if any, world sportsmen have attracted as much attention or focus. And he was coming to New Zealand while at his peak, not like Ali who had turned on an exhibition at Western Springs when far past his best.

Woods was secured only because his New Zealand caddy, Steve Williams, had a special affiliation with Paraparaumu. Steve had played the course as a kid and was keen to see if the master could tame the challenging links course. There is no question that, without Williams' influence, New Zealand would never have seen the Tiger.

It should have been a time for national rejoicing, a time when sports fans set aside their money and their holidays and headed for Paraparaumu. It wasn't. From the moment that the 'Second Coming' was announced, New Zealand was divided. In my opinion, it was all over the amount Tiger was reportedly paid for appearing, some $4 million. The worst elements of our egalitarian society emerged with a strong section of the media furious that he was being paid for one tournament what they couldn't make in a lifetime. Woods was portrayed as a greedy, grasping mercenary completely unjustified in cashing in on his talents. There's no question that this sparked a public backlash. People complained about the entrance fee, the venue, the security and about Woods not signing autographs. But most of all they grizzled about the amount he was being paid. The only group not complaining were those who had guaranteed Tiger's appearance fee.

The tournament was a disaster. Woods played poorly by his standards, although he still finished sixth. It rained a good deal and Greg Turner behaved petulantly after being refused entry to the course by an officious gatekeeper. The crowds stayed away and the organisers were shown up to be rookies.

Those who did embrace the tournament had an experience they would never forget. No one enjoyed it more than one Thomas Butler, a Maori grandfather from Kaitaia, who had responded to an advertisement calling for helpers. Why? 'Well, bro, I wanted to tell all the grandkids that Poppa had seen the world's greatest sportsman.'

The interview I did with Tom went some way to turning the tide of public criticism. Tom told the listeners that for the past week he had been sleeping on the back of his truck under a local bridge. What amazed me was that the people working with him all knew this but none invited him home, even if only for a meal. So for the remainder of the tournament, Tom stayed with me at the City Life Hotel and Newstalk ZB received a slightly inflated expense account. It evened out because Newstalk ZB got first-hand the best story of the tournament.

Michael Campbell is a likeable extrovert whose early larrikin tendencies have disappeared through the influence of his classy wife and the discipline and code of behaviour golf demands. Michael's generosity knows no boundaries and his gifts to Ronald McDonald houses and junior golf reflect his attitude to life. I've been privileged to interview him on a number of occasions, the most pleasant being at Kauri Cliffs, New Zealand's most scenic course.

My favourite golfer is Philip Tataurangi, partly because he was the first subject for the *Deaker Profiles*, a programme that ran for eight years on Sky. Philip, whose father Teroi was an exciting midfielder with Auckland in the 1960s, going desperately close to representing the All Blacks, is a rugby fanatic, who is always totally supportive of his beloved Waikato team and the All Blacks. It's impossible to complete an interview without giving him an insight into the latest rugby gossip.

Frank Nobilo has a reputation for being a difficult fellow to deal with. It's a reputation totally without justification. I've always found him to be polite, sincere and direct. In fact, it's his honesty that often gets him into trouble. He was justifiably annoyed at the amount of media attention that used to be directed towards Michael Campbell, not so much for his golfing achievements but more because of the fixation sections of the New Zealand media had with anything Maori.

For many years, Frank was our number one golfer but for most of it the media ignored him. I never saw Frank at his best but just before the 2003 Open he invited me to play a round with him at Middlemore where I witnessed a spectacular shot. On the par-four second he hit his drive to within 130 metres of the pin and took out a nine iron. His approach landed 4 metres past the pin where it gripped and ran back into the hole. The greenkeepers raking the bunkers burst into applause. Frank is now showing the same finesse in his commentaries that used to distinguish his performances in the world's major tournaments.

It's difficult to assess how popular golf is as a radio sport. We've always commanded a good audience for the New Zealand Open but we incurred our lowest-ever rating for the inaugural Clearwater Classic. Perhaps it was because the tournament was in Christchurch and poorly patronised. The event attracted a stronger field than usually turns out for most New Zealand Opens but the public seemed to be turned off because the names they were accustomed to weren't there.

Reece Bishop couldn't quite make it as a professional golfer though he did win the Noumea Open, 45 pro-am events and has been the top resident New Zealand professional for three of the past five years. He's now an outstanding coach. Probably no golfer has tested his patience and fortitude more than I have.

Like a lot of former cricketers, my long shots tended to slice. The longer the shot, the greater the slice. The problem, you see, is that cricketers play mostly off the front foot with their wrists 'unbroken' and the elbow up, while golfers 'break' their wrists like baseball batters and tuck the elbow away. It's been the hardest habit to drop.

Early in 2003 I was on the verge of giving the game away. I'd got my handicap down to 15 but from that point it wouldn't budge. No matter what I tried, my rounds still ranged between 87 and 95. Finally, someone said, 'Just hit it like you would a baseball', whereupon the penny dropped. Golf is never mastered. You're always learning. My current objective is to improve my short game, which I'm working on constantly. It's obviously the secret to low scoring. My current handicap is eight but I want to get it as low as five.

In 2003, I had the privilege of playing three holes in the company of Sir Bob Charles. On two of those holes I outdrove him, but after the three holes Sir Bob was two shots up on me. The man is a master of the short game. You have to admire his discipline and fitness. He doesn't carry one extra kilogram and is mentally and physically as sharp as could be. Over the years, since he achieved golfing immortality by winning the British Open, he's been an outstanding role model for New Zealand golfers.

New Zealand golfers have achieved on the tough, international circuit where our tennis players have failed. Much of the credit can be attributed to the administration skills of the late Grant Clements. This, together with his ability to get the best out of the gifted coach Mel Tongue, has been the secret of New Zealand's successes on the international stage. Mel is an absolute character, full of vitality and fun. At the same time, though, he knows the game and was clearly responsible for taming Michael Campbell and directing him down the right path. With Phil Aitken, a former New Zealand representative, also at the helm New Zealand golf was in good hands.

I've been fortunate in the support and encouragement I've received from people like Rick Ellis of Gulf Harbour and Eric Faesen Kloet of Premier Driving Range and the Golf Warehouse. Somehow, Eric arranged a complimentary set of Calloways for me and next to the Holden they're my favourite possession.

If I had been introduced to golf earlier I'm sure I would never have played cricket. In golf you're given a second chance, you're always the centre of the action and you can play on your handicap against any golfer in the world. No two rounds are the same, nor are any two shots, yet you need to follow the same discipline before every shot.

Most important, I've never met a bad person on a golf course. Golfers return the clubs they find and most don't rant or rave. And none of the individuals I've ever played with cheat by taking a better lie or deliberately modifying their score card.

A person I often think of when I'm playing golf is Lin Colling, the former All Black halfback and selector. Lin, Peter Griffiths and I used to play Gulf Harbour and Muriwai regularly. We learned the game together and as any golfer will tell you one of the most important elements in the game is club selection. Lin always used to say, 'When in doubt, choose a club that will give you greater distance but don't try to hit it too hard.' I'm often in doubt on the golf course and I always reflect on Lin's comments.

While Lin enjoyed golf, he was passionate about rugby. And the courage he demonstrated as a player with Otago, Auckland and the All Blacks remained with him through to his untimely death. Griff rang me one Monday morning to say that Lin was in Auckland Hospital but there was no point in visiting him because he was on his way out. Twenty-four hours later Griff phoned to announce that following a course of steroids, Lin had rallied. So I went to see him, not knowing what to expect.

Lin was out of his bed waiting for me. 'There's no bloody way I was going to let you see me lying there like an invalid,' he said. His doctor arrived and they went away for a serious chat. When Lin returned, he was chirpy and started foraging for his clothes. 'He's given me another month,' he said. 'That'll do. I'll be able to see the Blues win the Super 12 final.' Which he did.

Griff and I organised a charity golf tournament, with the proceeds benefiting junior rugby and epilepsy. The trophy played for was the Lin Colling Memorial. But blokes like Lin don't really need memorials. Those fortunate enough to have known him will never forget him. His courage was an inspiration to all of us.

That New Zealand is a golfing Mecca was graphically illustrated to me in January 2004. Richard Kahn, my usual playing partner at Gulf Harbour, announced he was heading for Queenstown to pick up a car that had to be delivered to Auckland and that he intended to play golf the whole way back.

'Who's going with you?' I enquired.

'I'm going on my own,' he replied.

'No, you're not. I'm coming.'

Two days later I was in Wanaka playing a delightful community course with special views of the lake. The green fee was $30. Anywhere else in the world there would have been no change from $100.

On to Queenstown's Kelvin Heights. If the views at Wanaka were special, those from Kelvin Heights were nothing short of breathtaking. Again, the fee was $30, which is ridiculously cheap. We drove up through Omarama, reaching the Lindis Pass around dusk. The views, highlighted by the awesome sight of Mount Cook, made us proud to be Kiwis. Surely the trek we were on would have huge appeal for overseas golfers.

It seemed a lifetime since I'd last arrived in a town for an overnight stay without making prior arrangements. We stayed at a bed and breakfast place in Geraldine for the princely sum of $40, the breakfast matching anything I've experienced at the finest hotels Newstalk ZB has booked me into while covering major sporting events around the globe.

The following morning we played Terrace Downs, a unique course set above the Rakaia Gorge with tussocks for rough. If any course offers a more environmentally suitable clubhouse I've yet to encounter it. Outstanding use has been made of stones from the Rakaia. Where else in the world can you sprawl back in a spa and overlook the 10th hole with stunning views of the mountains and river in behind? The green fee here is just $50.

My favourite Christchurch course is Shirley, with its established trees and sense of history. The club is lucky to have Shane Scott, the personable coach of Eddie Lee, as its professional, and all the staff follow his lead. When I rang to book a tee time, the young woman answering said, 'No problem. What's the name, sir?'

'Murray Deaker.'

'Sorry, sir, the course has just filled!' was the retort from an ardent Crusaders fan.

Our only disappointment was Paraparaumu, reputedly the country's top links course and rated among the top 100 courses in the world. Sadly, the entire place is in need of a facelift and the course has fallen into some disarray.

On the other hand, it would be difficult to find anything to criticise about Wairakei. It's arguably the best course in the country and owners Gary Lane, Trevor Farmer and Peter Francis are to be congratulated on providing golfers with a course that would grace any major tournament. Slightly more expensive at $60, it's still a bargain for a round.

In seven days we played seven rounds of golf on six courses that highlighted the best of New Zealand's varied landscape. Our golfing Mecca is waiting for a young entrepreneur to market it to the world. Throughout its length and breadth are wonderful courses available to the public for a pittance. In the Far North Kauri Cliffs, Kerikeri and Waitangi are hard to surpass while the new Cape Kidnappers course in Hawke's Bay is stunning. If I were 20 years younger I know what I'd be doing, especially if I could take a microphone with me.

Perhaps the greatest compliment I can pay golf is to conclude by saying that the only job I would trade the microphone in for would be a place on the Seniors Tour. Daydreams are free: I'm more likely to achieve successive holes in one.

Sponsors

It would be impossible to tally up the number of times a talkback caller, usually from a minor sport, has rung to ask, 'How do we get sponsors?' A more valid question would be, 'How do we hold onto sponsors?' Most sports bodies and individuals haven't a clue how to treat sponsors. Invariably, they'll take the cheque, spend it, do nothing for the sponsor and expect another cheque the following year.

The CEO of Sky Television, John Fellett, told my wife Sharon and me that our treatment of sponsors was light years ahead of anyone else in the media business. Perhaps it's a direct carry-over from our days working for the Foundation of Alcohol and Drug Education (FADE) and Life Education trusts. Neither of these organisations would have got off the ground without our ability to raise money from corporate sponsors. Both were like bottomless pits and in FADE's case, particularly, centred on an unpopular charity, teenage drug use.

We learned how to cold call, what to offer sponsors and how to deliver. Most of all, we appreciated how difficult it is to get corporates on board and consequently once we'd secured them, we did everything we could to keep them. We asked ourselves the key question: 'What can we do for them?'

Slightly less important is finding the right sponsor. When Mike Hutchinson was CEO of Saatchi & Saatchi he informed me that Sanitarium had been monitoring my programmes for some time and liked my values. The company is owned by the Seventh Day Adventist Church and produces a number of health foods, the best known of which is Weetbix. I'm not a churchgoer but I do have a strong faith. Since Sanitarium approved of my values and it was natural for a sports host to be promoting healthy foods, we met.

It's vital when meeting a sponsor or advertiser that you don't promise something you can't deliver. Sanitarium wanted to advertise on our television show, give away Weetbix on my radio show and associate my name with their product. We felt we could do a little bit more for them and Sharon suggested they use me to speak at staff functions. I've done this on about six occasions, and enjoyed it. We also suggested that their office and factory workers might like to come and view our live television show and many have taken advantage of the offer.

We endeavour to contact all our advertisers and sponsors at least once a fortnight. It may be a note in the mail, a fax or simply a phone call, but it's regular. Less often, I'll have lunch with representatives from one of the companies, always at the downtown Auckland restaurant of Seamart, another advertiser.

Most of my sponsors and advertisers have been with me many years, some, like Schofields, from the time I started on radio. I'm always looking for an angle on their behalf. The best I've come up with was the slogan associated with Alpers Seafood Bar and Grill.

Doug Page, a former freezing worker at Otahuhu, was one of the craftiest proprietors who ever drew breath. He wanted value for his advertising dollar and monitored the impact of each advertisement. If the ad didn't get the phones at Alpers ringing, he was quickly on the line to me. While in Boston on a Woolf Fisher Fellowship, I'd been taken to a rough diner down by the wharves. Since my host had put me up at the Marriott, I was somewhat surprised by his choice of eating place. He observed my reaction and said, 'Wait until you've tried the chowder here.' He ordered two pots of it, served from a huge cauldron, and promptly put his spoon in the middle of it. The spoon didn't move. He exclaimed, 'That's how you tell a good chowder. The spoon stays upright in the middle.'

John Yates, a member of the famous Yates rugby and league family from Northland, was the cook at Alpers. I began to advertise the place as having 'the chowder in which the spoon stands up in the middle'. After a week of advertising, I took the family to dinner there. When we walked in all the diners looked at me. Naturally, I ordered the chowder and when the spoon stayed upright in the middle, there was a spontaneous burst of applause. Doug Page, a difficult man to keep happy, could hardly contain himself as the average numbers eating in his restaurant per evening swelled from 19 into the sixties.

No sponsor has received greater value for money from me than Holden. To a large extent, Holder has piggy-backed on my relationship with Schofields, the sponsor of Sportstalk on ZB. Again, it's a perfect mix. I'm the kind of guy you would expect to drive a Holden. On a couple of occasions I've had approaches from BMW dealers, saying it was about time I moved up. My response has been constant: 'What, and ruin my image!'

Holden is an Australasian car, one we can all identify with, and one in which most Kiwis have had a variety of experiences. It's a car New Zealanders relate to — no frills, highly practical, plenty of grunt and ready for a challenge. I'll drive a Holden until the day I die. The plugs I give Holden during the build-up to Bathurst and Pukekohe are completely over the top. Greg Murphy plays along with it brilliantly, but almost lost it the time I referred to Ford as 'that other four-letter word beginning with F!'

If I'm invited to play golf on a corporate day, I'll think carefully about my choice of attire. The opportunity allows me to give one of my sponsors a plug. I rarely get caught out, though in 2003 at the Holden media day I had to change my cap. I was wearing a Holden shirt and an Air New Zealand cap, until I discovered that Emirates Air was the main sponsor for the day. A quick trip to the boot of my car saw the Air New Zealand cap replaced by a Holden one.

My longest association with a sponsor has been with Regency Duty Free. It had its origins in an address I delivered at the Pakuranga Rugby Club. Among the audience was Regency's CEO, Kelvin Ricketts, who approached me to ask if I had advertising space available on my programmes. Regency has been with me on radio for 10 years and on television for five years. Kelvin was very supportive when I was ill and when Regency's business took a dip because of the SARS virus, I dropped my advertising rates by 50 per cent. During the heady times for Regency, Kelvin invited Sharon and me to accompany him and his wife Mav to the Olympics in Sydney. We had an absolute ball and the event remains one of the highlights of my life.

Being involved with sponsors can also bring additional bonuses that dollars could never match. Kelvin dreamed up the Regency Duty Free Sports Foundation to help talented youngsters become future world champions. Regency and its suppliers provide the money and over four years 30 future champions have received more than $300,000. I've been privileged to be a member of the compact board that allocates the funding.

Weetbix triathlons give me a similar buzz. These are now staged all around New Zealand, catering annually for 15,000 kids. To see these young Kiwis giving it their best, supported by enthusiastic parents, is the sporting highlight of my year. One of my favourite photos shows me putting a ribbon with a Weetbix winner's badge on it around the neck of a delighted young girl.

Most clubs don't report back to sponsors about what they do on their behalf. My trip to the 1999 Rugby World Cup wouldn't have been possible without Air New Zealand. We negotiated a contra arrangement with them on the understanding that they would be given brief credits during my programmes. I kept an accurate record of the time of each mention and upon my return wrote to Air New Zealand, thanking them for their support and advising them they had received 138 mentions. Perhaps that had some influence on the airline becoming the major sponsor of my television show for four years.

Yet Keith Fong, the marketing executive responsible for building the relationship, assures me that most people take the free air trip and offer nothing in return. He has a wealth of stories about people who have abused the system, even to the extent of sports stars who have been given free trips subsequently advertising a rival airline.

All sponsors are looking for coverage and subtle, or not so subtle, reinforcement of their product. This can be achieved in a number of ways. If I'm giving the results from Bathurst or Pukekohe I will always say, 'First, Greg Murphy, driving his Holden.' I will always call the NPC the Air New Zealand NPC. The men's tennis at Stanley Street is always the Heineken Open. During the 2003 Rugby World Cup we negotiated an excellent accommodation deal that led to me introducing certain segments by saying, 'I'm broadcasting from the Avillion Hotel, corner of Pitt and Liverpool Streets in downtown Sydney.'

Sponsors are also looking for loyalty. I would never drive any car other than a Holden, would only fly with Air New Zealand, my duty-free shopping is only at Regency, I bank with the Bank of New Zealand, eat Weetbix for breakfast, buy only DB products for my friends to drink and always stay at the Avillion in Sydney.

Canon is another of my sponsors and if I'm referring to a collection of photographers, I'll say, 'All the country's top photographers are here today with their Canons.' The Canon Sharpshooter has become a major feature of my television show.

Sponsors will run a mile from controversy, as clearly illustrated by Mitsubishi withdrawing its million-dollar support of the *Holmes* television show after Paul uttered his infamous 'cheeky darkie' comments. Yet none of my sponsors threatened to bail out when I was taken off air in 2003. One advertiser asked for a reduction in the rate he paid while all the others contacted Sharon offering help and sympathy. Loyalty is a two-way street.

For sponsorships or advertisements to work, they need to be presented with enthusiasm, genuineness, directness and honesty. Biomag, the magnetic underlay that fits over a mattress, can bring some pain relief. Sharon and I have been sleeping on one for more than two years and it has given me relief from back pain. I admit this on air and people obviously believe me because when I do the advertisement Biomag sells 300 per cent more of its product than when any of my replacements do the same ad in the same time slot.

If you treat sponsors well, they become part of your organisation. This was vividly illustrated in late 2003 when we contacted Air New Zealand, DB Breweries, Holden, Canon and Regency Duty Free to determine if they wanted to remain as sponsors of the TV show in 2004. All reconfirmed their commitment over the phone. We lost only the Bank of New Zealand but they had given us a year's notice, advising their intention to spend their marketing dollar in a different way.

Fortunately, Tom Blackhurst, Mr Biomag, has developed such a strong relationship with me on radio that he jumped at the opportunity to introduce the concept 'Give that man a Biomag' to any person suffering a big hit. Those hits have led to some spectacular television footage and increased sales for Biomag.

Leighton Smith gave me the best piece of advice I could have received for dealing with advertisers and sponsors. 'Deaks,' he said, 'you must be squeaky clean, totally transparent. Declare everything you earn.' Leighton proffered that advice just as I was launching my career in broadcasting. At that time it was public knowledge that broadcasters sometimes indulged in contra arrangements. I was glad I listened to Leighton, for when Alan Jones and John Laws were caught up in the cash-for-comment scandal in Australia, the IRD suddenly became interested in New Zealand broadcasters. Fortunately, I had nothing to hide.

A peripheral benefit of building a family of sponsors is that the people you deal with become personal friends. I'm close to Kelvin Ricketts, play golf with Gary Walker of Canon, glean interesting information from Peter Wills of DB, argue and debate endlessly with Keith Fong of Air New Zealand and listen carefully to the insightful comments of Norm Thompson, anther dedicated Air New Zealand man.

Over the years I've come to value the judgment of Brian Blake, the CEO of DB Breweries. He's an astute, thoughtful businessman who consistently looks outside the square. In 2002, we invited all our major sponsors to a small luncheon at the City Life Hotel where a lively discussion, on a multitude of topics, ensued. I had to acknowledge that it wasn't an original concept: I'd borrowed the idea from a DB luncheon chaired by Brian.

The Mad Butcher used to sponsor any number of charities and clubs but to a large degree he's pulled back. 'Mate, they don't know how to say thanks,' he said, 'and none of them help me sell any more sausages.' In his own inimitable style he has summed up perfectly why so many clubs miss out on sponsorship: they are not appreciative and they don't give the sponsor anything in return.

The golden rules for sponsorship, that all clubs should apply, don't involve any rocket science.

1. Identify sponsors that can benefit through being associated with your club;
2. Outline clearly how your club will put the sponsor's name 'up in lights';
3. Insist that club members support that sponsor and advise the sponsor they belong to the club;
4. Get the sponsor involved in club activities — prizegiving, free tickets, invitations to events;
5. Remember that your club can never say thank you too often;
6. Keep the sponsor informed by newsletter, personal notes, faxes and phone calls;
7. Acknowledge the sponsorship formally with a plaque, badge or memento suitable for display in the sponsorship company's reception area;

8. Visit the sponsor personally at his office twice a year;
9. Refer any business to the sponsor and let the sponsor know of the potential customer;
10. Take the key people out to lunch at least once a year.

The clubs who are guilty of rudeness and intolerance towards their sponsors should take a leaf out of world junior duathlon and triathlon champion Terenzo Bozzone. He gets his shirts printed with the names of all his sponsors on them. He has his own web page acknowledging his sponsors and he's consistently emailing news to them. Perhaps that's why he has received more than $25,000 from the Regency Duty Free Sports Foundation.

Motor racing

Motor racing enjoys an extraordinary following in New Zealand. If 91,000 people can turn up to Pukekohe over three days for a V8 Supercar race, there's an incredible number of petrol-heads in our society.

If that doesn't convince you, count the number of Holden jackets being worn at the shopping centre or at Big Boys' Toys next time you're there. The amazing thing is that most in the media just don't realise or understand what a following the sport has. Any time I've interviewed a driver on radio, the talkback line is crammed with callers and you don't get that with some of the supposed 'high-profile' sports in New Zealand.

To quantify that even further, motor racing has produced an unusually high number of international achievers, given our population base — and not just on the track. The number of mechanics and IT specialist in Formula One and other formula overseas is testament to how highly regarded a New Zealand accent is in Europe and the United States.

Few other sports can claim the fame levels of the 'Trio at the Top', Bruce McLaren, Denny Hulme and Chris Amon. What they achieved worldwide has still not been emulated by any other New Zealanders, and very few other nationalities. Few men in the world have won a Grand Prix in a car of their own design as Bruce McLaren did at the ridiculously young age of 22. It's only in the past year that his 44-year record of being the youngest driver ever to win a Grand Prix was eclipsed by rising Spanish star Fernando Alonzo. McLaren and Amon won the controversial Le Mans in the Ford GT40 with Denny Hulme second. In Can Am, the 'Bruce and Denny Show' made household names of McLaren and Hulme. No one else from New Zealand has reached that level of recognition in North America, though Scott Dixon's nearly there.

The curious thing is that none of these racing drivers was as famous in their own country at the time. Part of the reason could be the lack of television when they were competitors. Still, they were superstars nearly everywhere else and the comparative lack of recognition in New Zealand rankled with Denny Hulme, in particular; he wasn't called 'The Bear' for nothing. He grumbled endlessly about not being met by officials at the airport when he arrived back home after winning the world championship. Even after he retired to Lake Rotoiti in 1975, it used to piss him off no end to have to ask the promoters for tickets for a major event. In all other countries in the world, it would be de rigueur, not to mention respectful, for these things to happen to the world champion as a matter of course. Yet a number of officials in the sport would whisper behind Denny's back that he had 'a chip on his shoulder'. Maybe he did. Perhaps it was justified.

Bruce McLaren died too young to have the chance to be officially recognised by his country. Hulme received an OBE just four months before he died. When he received the letter confirming the honour, he apparently burst into tears. The request for consideration for this honour was initiated by David Lange, who has always maintained an interest in motor racing and would have to be one of the few prime ministers in the world ever to indulge in the sport. He raced a Ford Laser for one season and always maintained he got better publicity for coming last in a motor race than he did for coming first as PM. Chris Amon received an MBE over 10 years ago.

Our next best prospect in Formula One is, of course, Australian-born Scott Dixon. He was actually conceived (according to his mother) in the gem fields of northern Queensland in a place called Sapphire, but he arrived here at a young age and all his early motor racing success, and the crucial financial help that allowed him to become established overseas, first in Australia and then in the United States, is entirely made in New Zealand. There's no doubt that Scott is destined for Formula One, but if an appropriate offer isn't forthcoming, he may well stay in the States. By all accounts, he's a star in America, making huge amounts of money in a team he's happy with.

In November 2003 Scott Dixon bought back the company that was formed to kick-start him on the road to Formula One. He repaid the shareholders who'd had faith in him in the beginning. It wasn't the money they made out of the deal (described by one shareholder as being 'only slightly better than current bank interest rates'), it was the satisfaction they derived from putting him literally on the right track.

It's never been easy for Scott Dixon to talk to media and on occasions it's been difficult for media to talk to Scott. He's not averse to sighing when he's about to go on air, or to be heard grizzling in the background about the need to be interviewed, but dig a little further and he can exhibit a fine intelligence and an endearing wit. Not all media have the time or patience to persevere past this initial reluctance and discover this core.

Scott's mother acts as his media manager in New Zealand and can exhibit the same degree of nonchalance with the media when she's booking interview times, but she's quite happy to be interviewed herself. It would be a pity if Scott and his family forget his New Zealand connections when he moves on to greater things but, if he makes the grade in Formula One, he may grow out of this diffidence.

Denny Hulme didn't have the greatest patience with media either. Eoin Young, one of New Zealand's most successful international journalists, relates the story about Hulme in the United States being granted an interview with an important American media person. In essence, Hulme told the journalist he didn't know what he was talking about and to 'fuck off'. Eoin, who had set up the interview, was mortified. 'Denny came back into the trailer and I asked him what the hell he was doing. He just grinned and giggled in his characteristic high-pitched manner and said he'd go outside again and speak to the guy. He did and proceeded to give the journalist one of the best interviews I'd ever heard.'

Scott Dixon might learn those types of ropes, or he may not. The worry is he may be thoroughly managed out of spontaneity.

I interviewed Jacques Villeneuve when he had just won the world Formula One championship. Actually, I'd never heard of him before: I thought Villeneuve might be a brand of cigar or a bottle of wine. Richard Becht arranged the interview and I was given four and a half minutes on satellite. Interviews like this are organised for several media around the world and they're on a strict timetable.

My opening question didn't have anything to do with motor sport at all: I simply asked him what colour of dye he used in his hair! Thankfully, he couldn't see me to ask about my hair but he was nonplussed by the question that actually brought on a bit of a giggle. When my time was up, I was getting into my stride and carried on. The next minute a voice comes down the line: 'What the hell do you think you are doing?' And someone was also shouting abuse in French. It was apparently a producer at headquarters telling me I'd exceeded my time limit. The people in the control room at Television New Zealand must have wet themselves at all this nonsense. But that, apparently, was that.

The only other Formula One driver I've interviewed was Heinz-Harald Frentzen. Castrol brought him to New Zealand and the interview was teed up for *Deaker Profiles* and conducted in a lounge area of the Sky City Hotel. As a matter of interest, Heinz-Harald's father makes coffins but I'm sure that had no bearing on him being a racing driver.

My first impression of Frentzen was that the bloke was a jockey. Intriguingly, his girlfriend (or his wife, I'm not quite sure which) was a good 8 inches or so taller, but that seems to be the way with a number of stars in motor racing. Formula One supreme Bernie Ecclestone is a case in point. His wife is a former Swedish model and she's about a foot taller than him. Most of the media, young blokes in their thirties but older ones too, tend to drool over these women while their men, the achievers, stand quietly by and allow them to dribble. Very few 'Formula One women' actually have a role other than to be Formula One women but the media seem to lap it up all the same. My other main impression of Heinz-Harald Frentzen was the size of his forearms. It must come from battling all those G-forces. Denny Hulme also had forearms the size of tree trunks but, unlike Frentzen, he had the stature to go with it.

Sandy Myhre had set about 20 questions for him because I make no secret of the fact that I don't know much about motor sport. The problem was Mr Frentzen didn't actually speak English too well and I'm not sure he grasped the New Zealand dialect either. We struggled a bit through the interview and then it came to the final question. Sandy might have had personal reasons for asking this, but she included the question, 'How do you handle all the pit poppies in the sport?' So I duly asked it.

165

Now either Heinz-Harald was deaf and didn't hear the question, or he was blind and couldn't read my lips. The third option was that he'd conveniently chosen to completely ignore it. He blinked his eyes a couple of times and didn't appear to have the faintest clue what I was talking about. To be honest, I didn't have the faintest clue what I was talking about either. And quite what Castrol made of the whole thing has never been recorded. Interestingly, he hasn't had nearly the success on the track since that time and I prefer to believe it has nothing to do with me asking him about the girls in the pit lane.

Of all the sports stars I've met or interviewed over the years there are three who stand out for their ability to handle the media well and give sponsors wonderful value for money. They are Sir Peter Blake, Grant Dalton and Greg Murphy.

Greg Murphy is effervescent, even energetic to the point of being on overload, but he can relate just as easily to the most ardent Westie petrol-head as he can to the Colin Giltraps of the world. He was well trained by another consummate media professional, Peter Brock, who taught him so well that even if Murph couldn't race to the high standard he demands of himself, he would still understand what media and sponsor commitments are all about. Murph handles all his own management. Partly because of this, he knows the value of a good sound bite and he will go to extraordinary lengths to make himself available, and he comes across brilliantly on the box or the wireless.

By way of comparison, Marcus Ambrose, who pipped Murphy at the last round at Eastern Creek for the Australian V8 Supercar championship in 2003, first defers to the team's media manager. The latter is a wonderfully witty character who's been on Newstalk ZB a number of times, is built like the proverbial brick out-house and goes by the Aussie-originated moniker of Crusher Murray. When Crusher gives the go-ahead, Ambrose then asks his personal manager who decides, often on the spur of the moment, if an interview might or might not be appropriate. It's an arduous process. Some would call it bullshit. And some media people like Brian Kelly prefer to avoid the procedure altogether. It's undoubtedly why, despite being the current V8 Supercar champion, Marcus Ambrose isn't as sought after by the media as Greg Murphy. There's surely a lesson in there.

To give you another idea of how accessible Murphy is, I've interviewed him just minutes before he's about to fling a V8 around the track in a race that has the championship riding on it. Within a minute of his finishing, Sandy Myhre or Brian Kelly rush up to him with a mobile phone. Greg has just completed the equivalent of running a marathon or playing 80 minutes of full-on rugby, but he never seems to say no. And that's in spite of the fact that television think they have rights over him because they're paid to be there. It's extraordinary. Can you imagine John Mitchell or some of the All Blacks being so available or so acutely aware of the sponsors' needs?

At each of the first three V8 Supercar events in Auckland, Murph was the first driver to turn up. He flew in on the Sunday night and on the Monday before the race he was ready for the media. As a result, he captured a huge proportion of the early publicity and the surprise is that no other driver realised what he'd done. Even in 2003, the majority of the other teams and drivers didn't arrive in the country until the Wednesday. The fact that the boy from Hawke's Bay won each of the three rounds was the cream on the cake but he did the PR donkey work so thoroughly and efficiently beforehand that even if he hadn't achieved the remarkable three in a row, he had put himself out there.

Murph's a natural behind the microphone and unafraid to wear his heart on his sleeve, both of which contribute to his huge fan base here and across the ditch, though I believe he's been given a rotten deal over the years by the Australian media. He has character and he's a fine New Zealander, full of humour and spontaneity and with a zest for life. Above all else, he hangs in there. Even when he didn't have a driving job, he made himself available to the media as a commentator. It wasn't what he wanted but he did what he had to at the time. And that demonstrates incredible mettle.

If successful Kiwis like Greg Murphy, Jason Richards, Craig Baird and Paul Radisich weren't full-time racing drivers, they could each develop a healthy career advising other sports people how to deal with the media. Their off-track skills are superb and can possibly be traced to the fact that racing drivers grow up with a healthy understanding and respect for the value of sponsorship simply because they need it to follow their dreams.

Not every racing driver is like these Kiwis. It used to be said of Nigel Mansell that he moaned when he won, though I never got the opportunity to interview him and find out for myself. Some of the motor sport media still call a whine, or a whinge, the 'Mansell Syndrome' but at present New Zealand is blessed with a group of racing drivers who are so professional in their attitude that we're spoilt for choice when it comes to interview time.

Here's a prime example. Jason Richards rolled his car at Pukekohe on the Friday of practice for the V8 Supercars in 2003 and it couldn't be mended in time for the race. Instead of sitting back and grizzling about his fate or blaming everyone but himself, he took advantage of his availability. He helped with Brian Kelly's commentary for Newstalk ZB on the Saturday and on the Sunday he was comments man for the PA address system at the track. My producer, Greg Billings, says Jason Richards was one of the best commentators motor sport has had in a long time.

Furthermore, on the Sunday, when Richards wasn't available, Brian and Sandy hauled in Mark Pedersen from the New Zealand V8 touring cars to add the professional comments about our own series. He proved to be an astute observer of the sport and a marvellous addition to the broadcast team. He knew what he wanted to say and said it with authority and panache. It's hard to imagine any other sport that can readily call on such expert opinion given literally, freely and so competently.

On the subject of the consummate professional, the loss to rallying of Possum Bourne in 2003 was immeasurable. Not only did the sport have to farewell its most successful contestant, the country lost a sporting icon and the media lost a superb interview subject. The outpouring of grief following his death was extraordinary and due as much to Possum's invigorating character and media skills as his undoubted superb racing talent. If ever anything epitomised New Zealanders' love of motor racing, surely it was Possum Bourne's death: the mountain of flowers on his car outside his workshop in Pukekohe, the sheer number of messages posted on the website which outweighed those on Peter Blake's website after his death by two to one, the enormous crowds at his funeral. He has left a huge gap.

Of the drivers who live in New Zealand, the most fascinating is the redoubtable Kenny Smith. Anyone still racing at the age of 62 after a quadruple heart bypass and competing against sharp young 'hot shoes' no older than 16, must possess fortitude, courage and a sheer love of the sport. Kenny has the looks and stature of a jockey, a bit like Heinz-Harald Frentzen, and in fact he's been involved in horse trading and breeding among many other things in his life. He's been known to say that he feels more at home talking to his horses than he does to people. He might have specifically been referring to motor racing officials.

It's no secret that Kenny and officialdom haven't always been the most comfortable of bedfellows and over his long career he's crossed swords with those who run the sport, not just when he disagrees with the penalties being invoked on 'driver misdemeanours' but also on the way the sport has evolved.

At times Kenny has gone to the United States at his own expense to try to negotiate with drivers to come to New Zealand. But officials of the sport have stymied his efforts and the result has been a less-than-exciting formula competing for the prestigious New Zealand Grand Prix.

As things stand at present, the Grand Prix is run for Formula Fords at a track that's as close to the Antarctic as it's possible to get — Teretonga in Invercargill. Not everyone agrees with this, though the irony is that Kenny Smith thinks it's OK. Even at his age, he's trying to win the one championship that's eluded him to date, Formula Ford, so he's ruthlessly pragmatic about his own needs. Kenny's graphic language is an accepted part of his persona. When Sandy Myhre interviewed him for her book she said she got four hours with Kenny but when the expletives were deleted it was half an hour.

Ken Smith is trustworthy, calculating and quick on the track, and sometimes fiery off it. On more than one occasion he's been fined or reprimanded for threatening drivers in the pits after the race for real or imagined on-track antics. Still, more people respect his opinion, even if it's delivered with traditional redheaded ferocity. After all, he's won the New Zealand Grand Prix, he's competed overseas in Australia and Asia (often with his closest friend Graeme Lawrence) and, more recently, he's encouraged a growing number of young drivers, including Scott Dixon, Matt Halliday and the incredibly youthful but awesomely talented Hartley brothers.

Most glamorous racing drivers have equally glamorous wives and girlfriends. Kenny, too, is surrounded by women but the difference here is that Kenny's girls are related to him. His family consists of mother Dorothy (always in the pits with her ever-present handbag), sister Maureen, niece Karen (who is the on-track laptop computer expert) and great-niece Michelle, who, incidentally, is Matt Halliday's long-time girlfriend.

These women are the face of the Smith team and in spite of Kenny's numerous spats with officials over the years, the entire family was awarded the Keys to the Circuits, which allow them all free entry to every circuit in the country in perpetuity — the only team or family ever to receive this type of accolade. It came after Kenny was deservedly awarded the MBE for his services to motor sport.

In international terms, New Zealand motor racing is in good heart. Apart from Scott Dixon, there's Matthew Halliday, James Cressey, Daniel Gaunt and Wade Cunningham, all young and talented and all with the potential to race overseas and progress. This healthy state of affairs owes more to people who brought business nous and money to the potential CVs of these young drivers, like Ken Smith, Peter (PJ) Johnston, Craig Harris, Colin Giltrap and the McLaren Trust and others, than to the sport's governing body (even if the governors of the sport tend to bask in any real or potential vicarious glory). It's worth remembering, for example, that when Scott Dixon went to the managers of the sport for funding to get to Australia in the early days, he was told he was 'dreaming'.

In spite of that, there's talent aplenty in this country to continue the legacy left by McLaren, Hulme and Amon. The domestic series is dominated by the exciting V8 touring cars modelled on the highly successful Australian V8s.

There's some disquiet, however, about the incestuousness of officials being heavily involved in the promotion and merchandising of the New Zealand V8s. Many argue that they should stick to officialdom and not try to crowbar themselves into a successful formula. But with driver representatives (some of them very successful businesspeople like Mike Pero) on the board of the V8 promotion company, these officials may be reined in when necessary. At least, that's the hope because with 35 cars on the grid, it's an exciting spectacle that no one wants to lose through incompetent management.

That brings up the question of circuits. Per head of population, New Zealand has more racetracks than just about any other country in the world. Some of them, like Teretonga, are great drivers' circuits but have utterly abysmal infrastructure. A media room the size of the average toilet without a window isn't a good omen. And given that this is the 21st century, neither is having to tie bits of paper on to a piece of string and watch as it's hauled up one floor in the officials' building in

Invercargill. If that's not bad enough, cellphone signals tend to skip off the end of the track and head towards Antarctica.

If you talk to Brian Kelly or Sandy Myhre they have numerous stories about the difficulties of broadcasting from motor racing tracks. You might assume these two, like many of the correspondents for *Scoreboard*, have sophisticated broadcasting equipment — microphones, tapes, links to the studio — but the truth is they do it all from a mobile phone.

Some officials could take a leaf out of the drivers' book on media etiquette. Brian Kelly's been told off for speaking too loudly and Sandy Myhre was told she could do the coverage from the Jenian Homes Building at Pukekohe on the proviso she was 'quiet'. This is a reasonably tall order for someone delivering a radio report.

At Bathurst one year, Sandy was having trouble hearing her cues from me, so she ran into one of the pit garages and found a wardrobe that was sufficiently enclosed for her to hear what was being said in the studio back in Auckland. She levered herself in there with the door slightly open. With the lap times on her knee, a finger in one ear and mobile to the other ear, she started her spiel. Unfortunately for her, Tony Longhurst came along and shut the wardrobe door, which gave a whole new meaning to the media being kept in the dark.

When Brian Kelly made his first trip to Melbourne for the Formula One Grand Prix, there was no live television coverage so the only electronic media coverage was on radio. Newstalk ZB and Radio Sport didn't have the huge budget Bernie Ecclestone requires electronic media to pay for the privilege of covering his event, so another way had to be found to keep listeners up to date.

Brian hauled in Paul Radisich to help him with commentating from the Shell hospitality suite. The room was full of corporate people from all round the world and here were these two Kiwis, standing on a couple of chairs so they could see the track, yelling into mobile phones. Well, make that one phone. Brian and Paul passed it between them for the entire hour and a half it took to run the race.

Then there's the vexed question of the country's largest track near our biggest population base — Pukekohe. The V8 Supercars have a contract until 2005. Pukekohe Park Raceway has the licence with Franklin Racing Club (the horse people) to run motor racing at the track until 2022. However, it's widely known that the horse people are taking up more land and Eric Watson proposes to build some stables there and use the horse facilities as a training track. So it remains to be seen whether horses and cars can continue to share each other's patch at national and international level. And quite where the Australia V8 Supercars will go if Pukekohe's contract isn't renewed is open to speculation.

The only other circuit hosting these cars outside Australia is Shanghai. The Chinese are prepared to make their visit very profitable indeed whereas New Zealand simply can't afford to compete with the sort of money on offer there. What New Zealand does have, however, is an enthusiasm for the sport rarely seen at Australian tracks. Nowhere across the Tasman do 28,000 people turn up for the first practice session, as happened on the Friday of Pukekohe in 2003. Pukekohe's ageing track's infrastructure is 40 years old and would be hard pressed to cope with any more people than the numbers who turned out for the V8s. Remember, this isn't a world championship: it's the New Zealand round of a domestic Australian series.

There's considerable talk of a street race around the CBD in Auckland. It will be interesting to see whether Councillor Scott Milne can drive this project through the considerable opposition he has at the time of writing. The promoter, IMG, believes it will get the necessary sponsorship to build the circuit, so by 2006 the V9 Supercars could be flying around Fanshawe and Quay Streets and, with a bit of luck, I'll be able to see them out of the studio window.

If Scott Dixon races into Formula One in the next couple of years and if Greg Murphy and others continue to be adored by the public, motor racing might well out-muscle rugby and cricket in the news priority schedule. The long history of the sport in this country and the world success of a remarkably large number of participants could ensure this happens. More than a few people certainly hope so.

The Mad Butcher

Peter Leitch is the sanest person I know, yet he's made himself a multi-millionaire by promoting the perception that he's mad. At times he promotes himself so successfully that you would think he was nuttier than a fruitcake.

The Mad Butcher is to rugby league what Nelson Mandela was to the ANC, what Clint Eastwood was to spaghetti westerns and what Todd Blackadder was to Canterbury rugby. Yet the Butcher's knowledge of league could be put on a kicking tee and there would still be room for the ball. He knows as much about league as Winston Peters knows about humility and as Russell Coutts knows about loyalty.

What the Butcher does know heaps about is people. He reads them better than anyone I know. He's shrewd, cunning, manipulative, direct and honest. Most of all, the Butcher is an enigma. He can be charming, polite, urbane and delightful one moment and rude, blunt, coarse, earthy and basic the next. If you're a friend of the Butcher, you're a friend for life. Nothing is too much trouble and he will go to any lengths to help his mates.

With the Butcher there are only two types of people — good blokes and complete pricks, good buggers and bastards, people with their feet on the ground and those 'with their head up their arse' (to have your 'head up your arse' is the ultimate insult the Butcher can dish out). He'd give the good blokes the shirt off his back and kick the pricks in the balls. There are no half-measures with him. People who cheat on the Butcher are never forgotten and they do so at their peril because Peter Charles Leitch has a memory that would make an elephant appear to be suffering from Alzheimer's. If you cheat on the

Butcher, he'll get you back. We're close mates. I know that if I ever got into serious trouble and ended up 'inside', the Butcher would first try to bail me out, second he would contact his 'mate' Helen Clark and if both these failed he would bribe the guards.

The Butcher is New Zealand's Mr Rugby League, the official ambassador of the New Zealand League and the 18th Warrior. Until recently he had his own Mad Butcher Lounge at Ericsson Stadium that rocked after every home game. The central character was, of course, the Butcher, who orchestrated all the fun and frivolity. Peter has his own unique repertoire. If he sees a bloke arrive with a wife who is obviously younger than him, he will yell, 'Do you bring your dad out often, lovey?'

The best performance I've ever seen from him was at a pre-match Bledisloe Cup function in Auckland. Australians hosted the event and we were among a group invited along by Waste Management. The MC made the fatal mistake of taking the mickey out of the All Black supporters. He'll never do it again. The Butcher was on his feet in an instant. He flipped out his wallet and counted out $500.

'Righto, you bloody mongrel,' he said, 'stick your money where your mouth is. I've got $500 to say the All Blacks will beat the Wallabies.'

The MC seemed in urgent need of a blood transfusion. The general manager of Waste Management realised he had a potentially embarrassing situation on his hands but he handled it with aplomb. Bringing the audience to attention, he announced that his company had hired an international celebrity at great expense as a surprise guest speaker.

Peter and I were sitting together and we looked around to try and identify the mystery guest when the GM announced, 'Our speaker is the star of radio and television, all the way from Porirua via Auckland . . . Peter Leitch, the Mad Butcher.' What followed was the best after-dinner speech I've ever heard. Completely ad-libbed, it was brilliantly delivered. He was merciless on the Aussies, and they loved it. He concluded by getting the scattering of Kiwis present to stand and sing the national anthem — with our hands on our hearts — followed by a raucous haka. Only the Butcher could have pulled it off.

Vodafone should sponsor the Butcher, not the Warriors. He must be the biggest user of a cellphone in the world, and he returns calls instantly, regardless of who's left the message. Sometimes it's a butcher who's bought too much meat and wants some cash. Other times it can be a sports fanatic simply ringing up to abuse him. 'Mate, they all think I'm a bloody idiot,' he says, 'but I live in a million-dollar pad on the beach. From their state houses, they're telling me how stupid I am!'

The Butcher's generosity knows no limits. His wealth could be immensely greater, as he's given away hundreds of thousands of dollars. He's also most generous with his time. A few years ago a friend who lived in Invercargill was dying of cancer. For months the Butcher visited him or shouted him flights to Auckland. He kept the Air New Zealand share price up almost single-handedly.

Peter supports dozens of charities, chairs his own Mad Butcher Trust and has been a huge supporter of Kidz First. He loves people, particularly children. In the early 1990s he felt his business was in trouble and he certainly had a cash-flow problem. He rang me in a distraught, emotional state; in fact, he was a bloody wreck. I dropped what I was doing and drove to the sausage factory at Manurewa. For once, his zest, optimism and exuberance were shattered but between us we restructured his finances, which wasn't really difficult to do. He's never forgotten.

Peter Leitch is not my best friend. Sharon is. But there aren't many ahead of him. He is the best of Kiwiana, a self-made millionaire, a wonderful family man and a benefactor to society. I'm proud to call him a mate.

Where to from here?

New Zealand sport is at a fascinating stage in its evolution from passionate amateurism, where everyone felt they owned it, to cynical professionalism where, in some instances, only one or two individuals own the team.

It isn't something New Zealanders are coping with easily, as the cricketers' threatened strike and the All Blacks' petulant behaviour over bonuses have shown. The players seem to want the best of both worlds, combining the commitment of amateurs with the pay of professionals. Our rugby players are constantly moaning about the growing number of games they have to play but compared with the NRL or any of the professional games in the United States, they don't know they're alive.

Of greater concern has been the acceptance of mediocrity not only in sport but in all aspects of New Zealand society. Unquestionably, this has been a by-product of an education system that fudges results, tries to make everyone equal and recognises neither winners nor losers. And this didn't happen by chance. It was the clear policy of the Post Primary Teachers' Association which came to be dominated by feisty feminist-lesbians in the late 1970s. This group not only influenced policy but successfully secured principals' jobs for its supporters.

When I began teaching in 1970, New Zealand state schools were the envy of the western world. Any kid who went to King's High, Burnside High, Rongotai College, Hamilton Boys' or Takapuna Grammar could expect to compete easily with those attending private schools. The latter were disadvantaged in many areas but in just three decades we've seen a total turnaround. Our state schools have become pupil-centred classrooms in which a multitude of useless, flaky subjects are taught.

We've witnessed the end of the teaching of classical languages, the replacement of history by social studies, the teaching of soft physical education and the introduction of what appears to be ethnic English. Worse still, social promotion, the abolition of School Certificate and the broad grading of Sixth Form Certificate have all taken away the challenge to succeed. Kids don't know what it's like to pass or fail, to win or lose. Everyone passes now and, as a result, no one wins. We've bred mice for the rat race.

The standard of behaviour compared with 30 years ago is appalling. Corporal punishment did have its down side but when it was abolished, what replaced it? Of the many hundreds who received a caning few, if any, were scared either figuratively or literally. It allowed the majority of the class to get on with the job, free of the disruption caused by one or two malcontents. The loss of discipline, and self-discipline, can be identified every weekend on almost every sportsground.

So can the soft, non-caring attitude to the outcome of a game. Why should you strive to win when you've been brought up with the doctrine that losing is just as good, if not better? In every close game in any sport between New Zealand and Australia, the Aussies almost always win. Their society recognises winners and encourages them.

A generation gap has developed on this issue. Susan Devoy gave Kiwis something to be proud of with her squash successes at the British Open and in the world championships. She now has four boys with a fair sprinkling of Devoy genes in them. They play soccer, are apparently fairly useful at the game and have always been ecstatic when scoring goals. The principal of their school sent a newsletter home to parents advising them to tell their children not to celebrate the scoring of goals because the boys in the other team could feel upset. He has obviously no idea how upset Susan was when she read that.

A mate of mine went along to watch his youngster compete in the school cross-country. He'd taken time off work to attend but was running late so the event had started when he arrived. He asked the teacher in charge who was winning. She dismissed him with, 'Oh, we don't have a winner here. They're all winners for running.'

Recently, there was a major controversy over the score not being kept in girls' netball matches. Apparently the kids all kept the scores themselves but there was no official winner or loser. We've now had two generations of our kids subjected to this drivel and it's had a dreadful effect. When the going gets tough, they back off. You can almost see them throw their arms in the air and exclaim, 'That's not fair.' Our sporting heritage has been sacrificed in the name of participation. The emphasis that Kiwis used to put on competition is a thing of the past.

It's not only the education system and outfits like Netball New Zealand that are responsible for this malaise; the Hillary Commission must also take a large share of the blame. It actually encouraged non-competition in children's sport for over 20 years. The Kiwi Sport programme was fine for introducing kids to sport but what was wrong with having winners and losers? I avoid Wellington with its grey bureaucrats because it's the headquarters of the political correctness that has hamstrung this nation. Those responsible for developing the philosophy behind much that came out of the Hillary Commission should be lined up against the Beehive and shot.

What must happen now is a return to realism, challenges for all and the reinstatement of winners and losers and results. If SPARC isn't prepared to champion this it should give the government back the $54 million it receives each year.

In December 2003, Nick Hill, the chief executive officer of SPARC, rang and we arranged to have lunch. I didn't hold back, criticising severely Nick's actions in naming seven sports to receive privileged treatment while failing to attack the equality malaise that has permeated our sport. I said he'd be lucky if 10 per cent of those eating in the restaurant had ever heard of SPARC. If he wanted to make an impact he should come out clearly as standing for excellence. Closely allied to that would be support for winning and losing. It will be interesting to see if he's prepared to guide his quasi-government department down a path all the other politically correct bureaucrats have avoided.

It should be clear by now that I believe we need a change in attitude, an embracing of success, if New Zealand sport is to progress on the world scene. We'll always produce the Danyon Loaders, the Rob Waddells, the Evers-Swindells and the Ben Fouhys who succeed despite the system, not because of it. However, unless our attitude in team sports hardens we'll continue to lose the close encounters and the big events.

The Regency Duty Free Sports Foundation has unashamedly confined the criteria for recipients of its grants to 'potential future world champions'. New Zealand needs to build on this by providing mentors to assist those with potential. Former greats like John Walker, Dick Quax, Dick Taylor, Erin Baker, Susan Devoy, Chris Dickson, Grant Dalton, Colin Meads, Bryan Williams, Valerie Young, Michael Jones, Howie Tamati, Sir Brian Lochore, Sir Bob Charles, Sir Richard Hadlee, Brian Fairlie, Brett Steven and Cory Hutchings should be involved in one-on-one mentoring of these potential champions. And this wouldn't need to be an expensive exercise. I doubt any of the former greats would want payment, given that they came through in an era when people gave their time for nothing.

The tidying-up of the front desk, the administration, of New Zealand sport is well overdue. It's to be hoped that all our sports learned from the NZRU's disastrous experiment of overstocking its board with corporate types. Unlike business, sport contains a large element of emotion; the heart is as important as the head.

By now there should be a blueprint available for governance. If there isn't SPARC should develop one. The specific responsibilities of the board need to be clearly outlined and the roles of chairmen, deputy chairmen and board members carefully specified. All board members must be made completely aware that they're accountable for the performances of their sport. Their role is to govern and to ensure that the organisation's objectives are achieved.

The CEO is clearly responsible for the day-to-day running of the sport, the management of it. This includes direct responsibility for all the staff, coaches and players. Few are qualified to do it. Most make a complete hash of it but the few who do succeed set their sport up for top performances.

Chris Doig and Martin Snedden have been more responsible for the success of the Black Caps than many of the players, even those like Stephen Fleming and Chris Cairns. Snedden's appointment direct from a family law practice where he had only limited management responsibilities highlights the importance of selecting people with brains, values and a background in the sport. And Doig headhunted Snedden without the assistance of a personnel consultancy company.

I would question the use of consultants in sporting appointments. A number of coaches who were interviewed by Sheffield Consultants for NZRU jobs felt that the interviewers were simply a distraction. They didn't know a thing about coaching or managing a rugby team but had too much power at appointment time. Certainly rugby followers felt that a number of those who missed out, John Boe for example, were clearly better qualified than some of those who won Super-12 appointments.

Surely experience and a coach's record should be the determining factors for any appointment. Sadly, they aren't. Too often the interview panel decides principally on what the candidates say or how they behave during the interview. When you stop to consider how stupid this is you begin to understand the ludicrous decisions some panels have made. What's often not considered is the thing that matters most — the winning record of the candidate in front of them. Nor is enough emphasis put on checking the validity of that record. That should be the job of the consultant.

Rather than leave these important appointments to people who have probably never played rugby in their lives, why not involve successful former players like Graham Mourie, Bryan Williams, Warwick Taylor and Graham Purvis, who know the appropriate questions to ask and, more important, know the people who should be asked? Until we have the right people and the correct procedures, we'll continue to make inappropriate choices. Frankly, the least important part of the appointment process should be the interview. The candidate's record must be scrutinised fully, by all means and methods available.

Did the NZRU look into Mitchell's spell at Sale? I doubt it. Had they done so, they would have foreseen many of the difficulties that were to emerge during his tenure with the All Blacks. Did they scrutinise his role as one of Clive Woodward's assistant coaches with England? Highly doubtful again. By appointing him too early they may have ruined the chance of a more experienced John Mitchell coaching the All Blacks in about 2010.

Whoever is doing the media training of our top athletes should join the Wellington bureaucrats against the wall at the Beehive. What should be a pleasant, enjoyable experience has become, at least as far as the All Blacks are concerned, a most demeaning exercise for all concerned — a giant one-hit session with a frenzied sea of journalists all trying to complete as many interviews as they can with a largely reluctant group of players.

The All Blacks have developed a distrust of, even a disdain for, the media. Let me spell it out: most All Blacks hate the media. I'm old enough to remember when interviewing the All Blacks was a pleasure. Now I dread it. On most occasions, it would be more productive if the journalist provided the answers as well as the questions. The trite rubbish they usually utter makes them appear both ignorant and arrogant. I don't care whether they like me or hate me but someone should tell them that my Saturday and Sunday *Scoreboard* programmes reach 150,000 listeners, which is a bigger crowd than any stadium can boast.

Annemarie Mains approached me two years ago to do a one-off media-training session with the Highlanders. The feedback she got was highly favourable, with the notable exception of Jeff Wilson. He sat in the back row throughout with his cap down over his eyes, giving the impression he was there under duress because I was there. But I'd like to think the change in Taine Randell's approach to the media originated in that session. Individuals like Kelvin Middleton and Byron Kelleher certainly took on board the central theme of just being you. Both have a refreshing spontaneity when talking to television straight after a game.

You can't compare the All Blacks and such personable sporting achievers as Terenzo Bozzone, Scott Dixon, Greg Murphy and Sarah Ulmer. They all recognise the importance of their sponsors' funding and know that representing themselves worthily on radio and television is part of the deal. Most of the All Blacks give the impression the sponsors and the public owe them something. Unless they lift their game the public will hear less and less from them. It's the NZRU's responsibility to ensure they receive effective, practical, comprehensive media training.

And it's just as vital that the fans must learn to be more discerning. The tendency is to react with knee-jerk speed to the latest dilemma or crisis. Constantly, we over-analyse our team without considering the potency of the opposition. This helps to explain why we were so eager, before the World Cup, to pass off the England team as Dad's Army instead of appreciating that it was a highly talented, sweetly tuned force that had been winning more than 90 per cent of its internationals.

The media plays a role in this. If I hear another twit on television disparagingly linking Jonny Wilkinson's name to dropped goals the next kick will be me putting my size-11 boot through the screen.

Wilkinson's skill levels, game awareness, ability to control a match and generalship are light years ahead of any other five-eighth in the world. We seem to have forgotten that the objective of the game is to score more points than the opposition.

The New Zealand sporting media must both entertain and inform the public. They're doing a reasonable job in the first role but they've been falling down on their other task. Much of this has to do with the compactness of the country. If you're critical, the interviews dry up. In my time, Martin Crowe, Jeff Wilson and Daniel Anderson have black-listed me. Crowe I can understand, Wilson I can't and Anderson is a complete mystery to me. All that happens is that you keep on talking about the person but not to them.

In this small country our sporting stars can sometimes be small-minded. But that doesn't excuse the print media who fail even to check into public records to search for a story.

Exclude Phil Taylor, a feature writer for the *New Zealand Herald*, from that criticism. He produced a series of articles on the David Tua split with Kevin Barry and Martin Pugh that cast the two managers in a bad light. My understanding is that Taylor has never interviewed Tua; instead, he's relied solely on public records to develop his story, which represents an outstanding example of investigative journalism.

Richard Boock is becoming a top-notch cricket writer. He knows the game well enough, having grown up in a cricket-loving family and captained Otago B for a number of years. Brother Stephen was one of the best spin bowlers New Zealand has produced. Richard writes fear-lessly, which inevitably results in his disturbing the foundations of New Zealand Cricket.

Sir Richard Hadlee became his favourite target and although at times Boock has gone over the top, his columns have always been thought-provoking. They've infuriated Sir Richard to such an extent that he summoned Boock to Cornwall Park in Auckland where John Knowles, the former head of TVNZ Sport, acted as a mediator. The knight's opening spell — he was always lethal with the new ball — apparently lasted seven minutes. A nonplussed Boock claimed his only regret was that he didn't have his tape recorder with him. Sir Richard rated the various New Zealand cricket writers. Boock wasn't mentioned, so he asked about his own status. 'You're at the bottom,' snapped Sir Richard. 'Just mud.' It would have been a fascinating encounter: the country's greatest cricketer doing his level best to flatten the country's best cricket writer. Fortunately, both seem to have put it behind them. Sir Richard continues to do a top job as chairman of selectors and Boock remains fearless in his criticism.

At one stage, Boock was in danger of having his media accreditation revoked. It was just before the Black Caps left on a tour of South Africa and he was advised the team had held a special meeting to discuss whether to blacklist him. Common sense prevailed and manager Jeff Crowe took Boock out for dinner after their arrival in South Africa to help soothe relationships.

Both stories highlight the smallness of our country and the preciousness of our leading sports performers. When you consider the kid-glove treatment they receive compared with their British, American and even Australian counterparts, you start to appreciate why they often fold when operating outside New Zealand.

Free-to-air coverage of sport on television in New Zealand is an absolute disgrace. TVNZ, for so many years the leader in this field, has virtually given up. Its coverage plummeted to an all-time low at the 2003 Rugby World Cup. Sadly, Keith Quinn, an excellent commentator in his heyday, was way off the pace, guilty of mistakes a novice would shrink away from. Identifying England's mighty captain Martin Johnson, most people's player of the tournament, as Martin Devlin following the epic final has become one of sport's greatest faux pas.

Fortunately, the work of Willie Lose and particularly the entry of John Hart and Grant Fox lifted the commentaries, but nothing could have lifted the previews or reviews. Probably for politically correct reasons a young Polynesian who fronts a kids' programme was given the job of previewing the games. If there's ever been a worse sports show on television anywhere in the world I haven't heard about it. The reviews did challenge it but most were missed because viewers had turned off.

If TVNZ is to be competitive in presenting live sport its entire sports department needs a major overhaul. In Bernadine Oliver-Kerby it possesses an outstanding news anchor and Wayne Hay has surprised with his talents. Otherwise, its sports coverage is a disgrace and in an organisation where heads topple quicker than a New Zealand batting line-up when they're facing Shoaib Akhtar, it's amazing the sports department has remained intact.

Game of Two Halves is exempt from this criticism: it's magic television. Marc Ellis brings out the best in the complex Mathew Ridge, and Mike King and Martin Devlin, both of whom seem to have photographic memories for sport, are gifted entertainers. *Game of Two Halves* is produced by Touchdown, part of Julie Christie's empire, so TVNZ sport can't take any of the credit. Therein may lie the solution for TVNZ: it should buy its programmes from independent producers who have to be razor-sharp to keep sponsors happy and ratings high.

Sadly, *Sports Café* has had its day. Without Ellis, the show would have died three years ago. It's been leading an unhealthy existence for some time and is now tedious viewing.

TV3 has never made any great impact in sport. Clint Brown and Howard Dobson battle on bravely but rarely have anything fresh to offer. Why they didn't decide to put a top current-events sports show on at 7 p.m. each weeknight to go head to head with *Holmes*, only their 'experts' in programming know. Into this void stepped Sky Sport and Kevin Cameron, the former TVNZ producer. It's a mark of his success that Sky, launched in 1990, now claims 550,000 subscribers. This extraordinary growth is due to the company following the Rupert Murdoch doctrine of showing old blockbuster movies and plenty of sport.

Sky basically has the rights to all sport worth televising, with the exception of netball. Their live sport rates through the roof for a pay-to-view channel and the network continues to go from success to success. It's also establishing a number of home-grown sports shows that are enjoying success. *Reunion,* fronted by Tony Johnson, makes good use of live footage and Tony has successfully made the transition from radio to television.

Deaker on Sport, Cricket Company, The Mantis and the Cricket are other regular shows. Sky has struggled to establish its new nightly half-hour sports programme, *365.* It will need to improve markedly to survive: both production and presentation leave a lot to be desired.

The future for Radio Sport seems assured but the quality of some of the programmes needs urgent attention. Martin Devlin, with his witty, enthusiastic, high-energy style, remains its trump card, but the station lacks variety with too many of the hosts interviewing the same guests only hours apart. The questions are so similar you're often not sure whether you're listening to the original show or the 'best of' wrap. In my opinion, Radio Sport needs to embrace recreation and minor sports more. This means featuring segments on shooting, mountain running, mountain biking, gliding, board sailing, yachting, bowls, croquet, tennis, badminton, table tennis, ice skating, curling, skiing . . . The list goes on and on.

And what about me? The depression and its aftermath took me to my knees. It was a terrifying, haunting experience that I don't ever want to repeat. I feel now that I'm often walking on eggshells, taking small tentative steps, frightened to let go and be myself. The rock-bottom day I couldn't get out of bed is still vividly with me.

Not only do I feel different; I'm treated differently, particularly by those close to me who don't want to see me crack again. Any natural high, outlandish comment, raucous laugh or fiery outburst, all behaviour natural to me, is treated with alarm and I don't have to be telepathic to read their minds. *Oh, God, there he goes again.*

My family, who bring me immense pleasure, have the highest priority in my life. Sharon features a lot in this story: she's my rock, my comforter and my confidante. The days of deep depression and extreme highs knocked us both around and tested our relationship. Would our marriage ever be the same? Unbelievably, it may even have become stronger.

My kids are great. I love all three of them and fortunately they seem to love me. James lives in San Francisco with his American wife Amy and was capped PhD at Stanford University. I'm sure I was the proudest dad there. It's great when your kids achieve something you couldn't have. Kate became engaged in 2004 and she and Geoff are planning to marry at Christmas. It's a delight to see her happy and contented alongside 'my Geoff'. John completed a Bachelor of Business Studies without missing a paper, which amazed me because I thought he only went to school to eat his lunch. He took some time to settle but now there's no holding him. He works for me as a researcher and writes articles for magazines such as *Player*. After he'd interviewed Inga Tuigamala, Inga delighted in ringing to say, 'John's better than you, old man!'

Second marriages are never easy and often kids cause most of the problems. Sharon's son Bart and daughter Emma have done everything they could to make it as easy as possible for me. Fortunately, I can still beat Bart at golf but I anticipate things turning nasty when he finds more time to practise.

As always, the radio is a relief for me. I feel more relaxed, yet more in control, behind the microphone than anywhere else. When the time comes for me to move on I know I'll miss it. I remain as passionate, as committed, as diligent and as enthusiastic about broadcasting as I ever have. In fact, it's my lifeline. Some people work to live. I live to work.